The Miraculous Novena

This Memorial Edition copy donated by:

_____

In Loving Memory of:

_____

who resided in:

_____

Please pray for the resting of their soul.

Thank You and May God Bless You.

What are Memorial Edition copies?

Memorial Editions of <u>The Miraculous 54 Day Rosary Novena to Our Lady</u> are copies that provide you with the opportunity to write in the name of a family member, friend, or stranger who has passed away, while also requesting that the reader pray for the resting of your family member or friend's soul.

Regular price Memorial Edition copies are for sale on amazon's websites in the United States, the United Kingdom, Germany, France, Italy, and Spain.

However, we want people to pray the Rosary, and we encourage people to pray for the souls of the deceased, especially for our loved ones.

So, we are offering lower cost books available to you.

Discounted copies of Memorial Editions are available at Great Point Publishing for a lower cost per book, while being able to order multiple copies at one time.

To order lower cost discounted copies please visit:

greatpointpublishing.com/rosary

We hope you enjoy the opportunity to give a copy of this book as a present to a friend, or family member, or leave it in a Church as a gift for anyone to take.

Together let's promote the Rosary.

Together let's change the world.

Thank you.

The Miraculous 54 Day Rosary Novena to Our Lady:

Daily Prayer Guide to Help You Finish the Miracle Novena

By: Christopher Hallenbeck

Great Point Publishing

Gloversville, NY

The Miraculous 54 Day Rosary Novena To Our Lady:
Daily Prayer Guide To Help You Finish The Miracle Novena
By: Christopher Hallenbeck

Copyright © 2019 Christopher Hallenbeck, Great Point Publishing, LLC. ALL RIGHTS RESERVED. No part of this book may be reproduced, stored in a retrieval system, or transmitted by any means without the written permission of the author.

Cover design by: Gareth Bobowski

Book design by: Christopher Hallenbeck

Back Cover Photo by: Amanda Fortman, photo taken at The Church of The Holy Spirit in Gloversville, NY

Back Cover Author Photo by: Jamin Clemente

To order additional copies of this title, contact your favorite local bookstore or visit *www.greatpointpublishing.com*

Paperback ISBN: 978-1-7333797-0-0

Printed in the United States of America

Nihl Obstat: *Rev. David R. LeFort, Vicar General*
Albany Diocese
Albany, NY
June 10, 2019

Published by: **Great Point Publishing, LLC.**
Gloversville, NY

Dedicated to Blessed Mother MARY

and Queen of the Holy Rosary

in devout memory of

My Grandparents

Salvatore "Sam" and Margaret Guarnier

TABLE OF CONTENTS

An Inspirational Rosary Novena Story from Gloversville, NY	1
Afterword: E-mail from Gregg Wilbur	15
The 15 Promises of Mary to Christians who Pray The Rosary	16
How to Pray The Rosary	18
How to remember what Rosary day you're on	20
The Miraculous 54 Day Rosary Novena	22
About The Author	91
Thanks and Acknowledgements	91
About Salvatore "Sam" Guarnier	92
About Margaret Guarnier	96
End Notes	100

Note: In obedience to the decree of Pope Urban VIII (1623-1644) and of other Supreme Pontiffs, the author begs to state that, in regard to what is herein narrated, no higher authority is claimed than that which is due to all authentic human testimony.

AN INSPIRATIONAL ROSARY NOVENA STORY FROM GLOVERSVILLE, NY
By: Christopher Hallenbeck

There are special times in our lives when both you and I welcome Christ into our daily routines. Some of these routines could be small random acts of kindness or displays of charity that you try to practice habitually. Other times they could be special major events or milestones in your life. The events that are probably coming to your mind immediately are moments when you have received one of the seven sacraments; right now you might be recalling your first communion, receiving the sacrament of confirmation, going to confession during Lent and Advent seasons, or perhaps you're recalling the day that you were married to your wife or husband.

Sacraments are easy for you to remember because, according to the Catechism of the Catholic Church, "Seated at the right hand of the Father" and pouring out the Holy Spirit on his Body which is the Church... the sacraments are effective, valuable, and successful signs of grace, instituted by Christ and entrusted to the Church, by which divine life is dispensed to us...the sacraments strengthen faith and express it (CCC 1084, 1131,1133)[1].

The story that I'm about to share is not a recollection of a specific time that I received a particular sacrament. Instead it is the story of how I was introduced to the 54 Day Rosary Novena, and the blessings it has brought into my life, my family's life, and the blessings that it can bring into your life too. This story is five years in the making, and it wasn't until very recently that I first began to share this story. It was very private. I didn't want anyone else to know what I had discovered or what I was doing, and also there wasn't really much a story to share at the time.

Never in my wildest dreams did I ever imagine what would be brought into my life and my family's life five years later. All of this thanks be to God. The inspirational story about the 54 Day Rosary Novena to Our Lady in Gloversville, NY is a story about a special time that involves prayer, a sacrament, and strengthened faith. I hope you enjoy the read.

During Christmas in 2010, I was stumped on what to get my Grandma for a Christmas present. She was 91 at the time, and had been a devout Catholic all of her life. I usually would get her favorite candy, the chocolate and nut candy called Turtles, for her for Christmas. However, Grandma's teeth were becoming fragile and so my mom suggested that I think of something else to get her instead. So, I brainstormed in hopes of finding the perfect Christmas gift for my Grandma. Then the light bulb clicked! I thought of the perfect Christmas gift for her.

I'll get my Grandma a new set of Rosary beads. I'd never gotten her a set of Rosary beads before. She was always praying the Rosary, plus it was a thoughtful, creative, and meaningful gift. It was perfect! I searched online, and saw these beautiful blue Rosary beads that contained a picture of the Miraculous Medal on it, and I ordered a set. When they arrived, they were a lot nicer in person than the pictures I saw online, and my curiosity kicked in: what did each bead mean?

I learned how to say the Rosary in church school, but that had been a long time ago. So I ordered another set of the same Rosary beads for myself, and when they arrived I googled how to pray the Rosary. Next, I read everything that I could find on the Rosary. After doing so, there were three things that stood out to me at the time, and they have still stuck with me today.

The first thing that stood out to me was that I discovered the 54 Day Rosary Novena, also known as the Miraculous 54 Day Rosary Novena. If you're wondering why it is called the 54 Day Rosary Novena, here is the story behind why we say this Rosary for exactly 54 days, and how it was introduced to the Church:

Church history teaches us that in 1884 an apparition of Our Lady of Pompeii occurred inside the house of Commander Agrelli, an Italian military officer in Naples, Italy. For thirteen months, Fortuna Agrelli, the daughter of the Commander, was very, very sick. She had been in great distress, experiencing dreadful sufferings, torturous cramps, and even near death. So serious was her illness that her case had been given-up as hopeless by the most celebrated physicians of the time.

In desperation, on February 16, 1884, the afflicted girl and her family began a novena of Rosaries. The Queen of the Holy Rosary favored her with an apparition on March 3rd. Mary, sitting upon a high throne, surrounded by luminous figures, held the divine Child on her lap, and in her hand a Rosary. The Virgin Mother and The Holy Infant were clad in gold embroidered garments. They were accompanied by St. Dominic and St. Catherine of Siena. The throne was profusely decorated with flowers; the beauty of Our Lady was marvelous. Mary looked upon the sufferer with maternal tenderness, and the patient Fortuna saluted Mary with the words:

> *"Queen of the Holy Rosary, be gracious to me; restore me to health! I have already prayed to thee in a novena, O Mary, but have not yet experienced thy aid. I am so anxious to be cured!"*
>
> *"Child,"* responded the Blessed Virgin, *"thou hast invoked me by various titles and hast always obtained favors from me. Now, since thou hast called me by that title so pleasing to me, 'Queen of the Holy Rosary,' I can no longer refuse the favor thou dost petition; for this name is most precious and dear to me. Make three novenas, and thou shalt obtain all."*

Once more the Queen of the Holy Rosary appeared to her and said,

> *"Whoever desires to obtain favors from me should make three novenas of the prayers of the Rosary, and three novenas in thanksgiving."*

Obedient to Our Lady's invitation, Fortuna and her family completed the six novenas whereupon the young girl Fortuna was restored to perfect health and her family was showered with many blessings.

Through her, Our Lady gave the world the miraculous devotion of the 54 day Rosary Novena.[2]

According to the Benedictine Convent of Perpetual Adoration in Clyde, Missouri, This miracle of the Rosary made a very deep impression on Pope Leo XIII, and greatly contributed to the fact that in so many circular letters he urged all Christians to love the Rosary and say it fervently.[2]

But, what's the reason behind you having to pray the Rosary for exactly 54 days?

The early Greeks had a penchant for abstract thinking, and they thought that numbers were the key to all knowledge. The first one who thought it all out was Pythagoras.[3]

Pythagoras was the first person to calculate the beautiful sounds of harmonies, and how notes sounded by chords make harmonic tones if the notes of the chords are all interrelated in simple numeric ratios. This is standard music theory knowledge that we still use today. Pythagoras also came up with Pythagorean Theorem. In case you don't remember it from grade school, this is the square of the hypotenuse of a right triangle is equal to the sum of the squares of the other two sides. Pythagoras also gave numbers religious meaning. Somehow he was able to discover that things weren't just measured by just a number, but somehow they were also caused by number, and Pythagoras also taught that you could see the mind of God at work by looking at the ways that numbers work.[3]

Many years after Pythagoras taught that numbers had a religious meaning, Saint Augustine lectured many times on the Gospel of John, Chapter 21, verses 1-14. During these lectures Saint Augustine would explain the significance, and importance of the symbolism of the 153 fish that were caught in the Sea of Tiberias when Jesus told the apostles to cast their nets to the right side of the boat. Catching 153 fish is a very specific number of fish. This is important because "He (Jesus) didn't say anything like that the previous time he directed their fishing (Lk 5:4); he had already told them that He intended for them to be fishers of men (Mt 4:19), and He described the Last Judgement in terms of taking the creatures to His right (Mt 25:31-46). So the fish in John 21 refer to people, and Saint Augustine said 'the number signifies thousands, and thousands...to be admitted into the Kingdom of Heaven.'"[3]

The reason he gives is because there are 10 Commandments that you have to follow to get into Heaven. However, no one keeps the Commandments by their own power. We need help, we all need the grace of God. The grace of God comes in terms of the sevenfold gifts of the Holy Spirit.

Saint Augustine teaches us that there is a need for the Spirit so that the Law can be fulfilled. So add 10 + 7. What do you get? ...17.

According to Saint Augustine, however, you can't take this as a lump sum. It is necessary to account for every detail included in the seven gifts of the Holy Spirit and also the Ten Commandments and all of their implications, so when you add all of the numbers from 1 to 17, guess what number you get?...153!

This calculation according to Saint Augustine was why Saint John was so specific about the number of 153 fish caught; it lets you derive a general principle of salvation from a specific detail![4] This is important because it helps teach us why we pray the 54 Day Rosary Novena for 54 Days. Each number in the Bible has a traditional meaning dating from the time of Pythagoras, and contains a definite symbolic value today.

The number 3 stands for everything that is perfect. In Hebrew, Greek, and Christian thought, the third unit, unites the halves of 2. It reconciles any tension implied, bringing things to finish, to completion, to perfection! For example, the truth that the Holy Spirit "proceeds from the Father, and the Son," completes the Trinity. When you have three of anything, you have all that there is, or at least enough. That's why in Mass we say "Holy, Holy, Holy..." thrice Holy is as Holy as anything can be. It brings things to finish, to completion, to perfection![3]

During the apparition in 1884, when the Blessed Mother said to Fortuna:

> *"Whoever desires to obtain favors from me should make three novenas of the prayers of the Rosary, and three novenas in thanksgiving."*

A Novena is a Roman Catholic period of prayer lasting nine consecutive days.[4]

The number 9 is important because when you multiply 3 times 3 your answer is 9. Therefore, 9 is a symbol of perfection multiplied by perfection.[4]

When Our Lady first tells Fortuna to make 3 novenas of the prayers, she's telling her to pray for 9 days consecutively 3 times, therefore she's praying for 27 days in petition for her favor.

After praying for 27 days in petition, Our Lady then instructs Fortuna to say 3 more novenas in thanksgiving. Thus, she's telling Fortuna to pray in thanksgiving for 9 days consecutively 3 times, or 27 more days in thanksgiving.

When you add the 3 novenas in petition (27 days total), plus three more novenas in thanksgiving for your favor (27 more days), this is how you get and why you pray for exactly 54 days total during the Miraculous 54 Day Rosary Novena.

In 1926, author Charles V. Lacey wrote that the 54 day Rosary Novena is "a laborious Novena, but a Novena of Love. You who are sincere will not find it too difficult, if you really wish to obtain your request. Should you not obtain the favor you seek, be assured that the Rosary Queen, who knows what each one stands most in need of, has heard your prayer. You will not have prayed in vain. No prayer ever went unheard. And Our Blessed Lady has never been known to fail. Look upon each Hail Mary as a rare and beautiful rose which you lay at Mary's feet. These spiritual roses, bound in a wreath with Spiritual Communions, will be a most pleasing and acceptable gift to her, and will bring down upon you special graces. If you would reach the innermost recesses of her heart, lavishly bedeck your wreath with spiritual diamonds holy communions. Then her joy will be unbounded, and she will open wide the channel of her choicest graces to you."[2]

After reading about the 54 Day Rosary Novena, I decided that this was what I needed to help me learn the Rosary. The daily calendar would help keep me on track learning and saying the Rosary every day, and I also really liked the story of the miracle that occurred for the Agrelli family in 1884.

You see, in November 2010, my family was in need of a miracle at the time as well, and I felt that praying the 54 Day Rosary Novena was at the best way that I could help them. After all the miraculous Rosary Novena helped the Agrelli family in their time of need in 1884, and I wondered, could it help my family as well in 2010?

When I first read about the 54 day Rosary Novena, my brother and his wife and been trying to have a baby for about 18 months prior. I said to myself, "This is perfect! I'll say a 54 Day Rosary Novena for Mike and Diana to have a baby, and I'll get a Scapular so my prayers are as effective as can be."

On December 1, 2010, I began to say the 54 day Rosary Novena.

I also ordered myself a Brown Scapular around the same time. The power of the Rosary and Brown Scapular working together was the second thing I discovered that stood out to me when I was reading and relearning about the Rosary.

When my scapular arrived, inside there was a brief note explaining the history of the Brown Scapular and also recommending that first time wearers of the Brown Scapular should have their scapular blessed. I called the rectory at my parish the next day, and I talked to Father Don Czelusniak.

I explained to him that I just had gotten a new scapular and I asked him if he could bless it for me. Father Don said, "I can't do it this week, but Father Rendell can meet you." So I called Father Rendell Torres, and he told me to meet him at the rectory at 9am on January 6, 2011. It was the first Thursday of the month.

I remember this day specifically, because after Father Rendell blessed my scapular he told me that I should stop by the Church later to attend Adoration. They have Adoration of the Blessed Sacrament every Thursday, and that prayers were very powerful before the Blessed Sacrament.

That was all that I needed to hear.

At the time I'd never been to Adoration of the Blessed Sacrament, but when Father Rendell said that prayers before the Blessed Sacrament were very powerful, I knew right there that I needed to stop by after work to pray my daily rosary before the Blessed Sacrament.

Later that day, I did exactly that. After I got out of work, I went back to the Church of the Holy Spirit in Gloversville to visit Adoration of the Blessed Sacrament. I remember specifically that as I walked through the church, my newly blessed Scapular felt alive with the Holy Spirit as I walked in through the front doors. I kneeled down and prayed the Rosary before the Blessed Sacrament, continuing on with my 54 Day Rosary Novena.

In the following months I would try my best to make sure I'd say my daily Rosary on the first Thursday of the month in front of the Blessed Sacrament.

54 days later, I finished my first 54 day Rosary Novena. My brother and his wife were still not expecting. I thought I messed up somehow.

The next day I started to pray another 54 Day Rosary Novena, same format, visiting Adoration of the Blessed Sacrament every first Thursday of the month, and again praying for my brother and his wife to have a baby.

54 days later, I finished my second 54 Day Rosary Novena. And once again, my brother and his wife were still not expecting.

The next day, 109 days after I first started praying the Rosary, I began a third 54 day Rosary Novena, once again with the same format: visiting the Blessed Sacrament every first Thursday, and praying for my brother and his wife to have a baby.

54 days later, I finished my third 54 Day Rosary Novena. And once again, my brother and his wife were still not expecting.

After 162 days of praying the Rosary, I kind of got sick of praying the 54 Day Rosary Novena, and I needed a break. But what I didn't stop doing was visiting the Blessed Sacrament every first Thursday of the month.

In August of 2011, my Grandma was diagnosed with cancer. The week after her diagnosis, it happened to be the first Thursday of the month of August, so I visited Adoration of the Blessed Sacrament. I wasn't expecting a miracle, but I prayed that my grandmother would be in the least amount of pain as possible, and that she wouldn't have to suffer. The following week she passed away. It was on a Thursday. I was able to visit her the Tuesday prior. It was a normal visit, sad as I think we both knew our time together on Earth was nearing the end, but it was a good visit. We talked as if it were any other visit, and just enjoyed each other's company one final time. I made plans to go see her the next day, but when I called her she said that she was tired and just needed to sleep. She passed away the next day, at her house, and as far as I knew she didn't suffer, and was in the least amount of pain as possible.

It was experiences like these, and others that I began to believe in the capabilities and the true presence of the Lord in the Eucharist at Adoration of the Blessed Sacrament, and also in the liturgy of the Catholic Mass. In the liturgy of the Catholic Mass we express our faith in the real presence of Christ under the species of bread and wine by, among other ways, genuflecting or bowing deeply as a sign of adoration of the Lord (CCC 1378)[1].

Eventually I also learned and began to understand that through the Rosary and Adoration, I would obtain everything I asked for, BUT only if it was compatible with the Lord's will, and if it was for the better benefit of my soul or the person's soul that I was praying for.

I learned also that just like it says in Ecclesiastes Chapter 3, Verse 1:

> *"There is an appointed time for everything, and there is a time for every event under heaven."*[5]

Including a time for birth.

On December 10, 2012, my brother Mike, and his wife Diana welcomed their new daughter, Lucy. She was born exactly 739 days after I began my first 54 Day Rosary Novena, asking the Blessed Mother to pray with me to ask God to bless my brother and his wife with a baby.

All of those Rosary prayers, and the prayers before while visiting Adoration of the Blessed Sacrament were not in vain. There really was a true presence of The Lord in the Eucharist. Finally, I learned that the Rosary prayers were compatible with the Lord's will, and Lucy truly is for the better benefit of my brother Mike's soul and his wife Diana's soul also. There really is an appointed time for everything, and there really is a time for every event under heaven.

About a year and a half later, during Spring Break 2014, I was in Gloversville, and Mike, Diana, and Lucy were on vacation together in Myrtle Beach, South Carolina. My brother sent me a picture text message. It was a photo of the three of them, Lucy was wearing a pink shirt that said, "I'm going to be a big sister."

A couple of months after that, I was at The Magic Kernel in Johnstown, NY, and I got another picture text message from my brother. They were at the doctor's office. The picture that he texted me was an ultrasound picture, containing the words "Baby A" and "Baby B". Mike and Diana were now expecting twins, Lucy was going to have two younger brothers, due December of 2014.

About 18 months prior to receiving this announcement from Mike and Diana, the Feast of Corpus Christi was celebrated on June 2, 2013. On this day the Church celebrates the institution of the Eucharist. This day also celebrated the beginning of Perpetual Eucharistic Adoration by the Fulton-Montgomery County Deanery at the Church of the Holy Spirit in Gloversville, NY. According to the Catechism of the Catholic Church, because Christ himself is present in the sacrament of the altar, he is to be honored with the worship of adoration. "To visit the Blessed Sacrament is...a proof of gratitude, an expression of love, and a duty of adoration toward Christ our Lord." (CCC 1418)[1].

When Mike and Diana made the announcement that they were expecting again, I had already been one of the volunteers who helps make sure that Adoration of the Blessed Sacrament is exposed 24/7 at the Church and helping ensure that there is an Adorer there every hour of the day. The only time that Perpetual Eucharistic Adoration does not occur at the Church during the week is when Mass is being celebrated, or there is a funeral.

On September 16, 2014, I got a phone call from my brother Kolin around 5:30 in the evening. Mike and Diana were on their way to the hospital; Diana's water just broke, and they were rushing her to Albany Medical Center!

Immediately after hearing this, I went to the church, attended Adoration, and said a Rosary for Mike, Diana, and the twins, asking the Blessed Mother to pray with me that everything would be OK that day for my brother, his wife, and the twins.

A few hours later, I got a call from my Mom that one of the twins was on his way, and they had to rush Diana into surgery.

Once again I came back to Adoration that night and I said another Rosary. There was another Adorer already there, I didn't know who it was at the time, but I later learned that his name was Gregg Wilbur. Before I started praying another Rosary for Mike, Diana, and the twins, I told Gregg that I had a family emergency and my phone might ring while I was there.

I was on the last Hail Mary bead when my brother Kolin texted me that the twins were born, both healthy, and both breathing mostly on their own. I turned to Gregg who was seated behind me at Adoration, and I told him what happened earlier, and told him about the news I just got from Kolin. Gregg said to me, "Oh my goodness, you're not going to believe this, but I have twin boys myself, they're both 8 years old now."

The next day, on September 17, I began another 54 day Rosary Novena asking the Blessed Mother to pray with me that the twins would come home from Albany Med NICU both happy, and healthy. 6 days after I finished that 54 day Rosary Novena, and exactly 60 days to the day after they were born, Mike and Diana were able to bring Jackson and Finley Hallenbeck home!

Eventually, once the twins were all home and settled, I got the opportunity to share this entire story with Diana; how I bought a Rosary for Grandma, then one for myself, and afterwards praying three 54 Day Rosary Novenas for Mike and her to have a baby.
Immediately after I told her this entire story, she made the connection that she now has three kids, smiling ear to ear, the first thing that Diana said to me in reply was:

"Thank you for only saying three."

In closing, I have three things that I'd like everyone to remember and learn from this story.

1. Father Rendell was right back in 2011. Prayers before the Blessed Sacrament are very powerful. And when you pray please remember that you will obtain what you ask for if it is compatible with the Lord's will, and if it is for the better benefit of your soul or the person's soul that you're praying for. In terms of the 54 Day Rosary Novena specifically, whether the prayer intention has been received or not after the first 27 days (3 Novenas), you must still say the 3 Rosary prayer Novenas (27 days) in Thanksgiving. Sometimes your prayers might be answered within 27 or 54 days, sometimes it could take 60 days or so, other times it might take 739 days, or maybe even longer. However long it takes for your prayers to be answered, please don't forget the capabilities and the true presence of the Lord in the Eucharist. Through the Rosary and Adoration, you will obtain everything you ask for, BUT again only if it is compatible with the Lord's will, and if it is for the better benefit of your soul or the person's soul that you are praying for. Lastly, as mentioned earlier: don't forget, "There is an appointed time for everything, and there is a time for every event under heaven." (ECC. 3:1).

2. On April 21, 2015 there was an article published on ewtnnews.com that told the story of a Nigerian Bishop named Bishop Oliver who was in his chapel last year at the end of 2014. The Bishop was in his chapel praying the Rosary before Adoration of the Blessed Sacrament when suddenly Jesus appeared. At first Jesus didn't say anything, but he extended a sword to the Bishop. Bishop Oliver reached for the sword, and as he went to grab it, the sword turned into a Rosary. Jesus then said to Bishop Oliver:

> "Boko Haram is gone. Boko Haram is gone. Boko Haram is gone."

In 2009 there was around 125,000 Catholics in Bishop Oliver's Dioceses in Nigeria, however after a surge of violence from the Islamist Extremist group called Boko Haram, today in 2015 there remains only 50-60 thousand Catholics left. It was clear to Bishop Oliver that what Jesus meant when he told him three times: "Boko Haram is gone." Jesus meant that with the power of the Rosary we would be able to expel Boko Haram.[6]

Please share this story from Nigeria with your friends, family, and parishes, and ask them to pray the Rosary with you for this petition that God, Jesus, and the Holy Spirit will help remove that dangers and persecution of Christians demonstrated by Boko Haram and ISIS. The Rosary that Bishop Oliver was praying, is the same one that you and I can pray also. If possible, I'd highly recommend praying the Rosary while attending Adoration of the Blessed Sacrament. Through praying the Rosary, attending Mass to celebrate the Eucharist, and visiting Adoration of the Blessed Sacrament not only will you have the opportunity to change your life, but together both you and I along with help from the Blessed Mother Mary can help change the world to make it a better place to live.

3. When you first started reading the inspirational story of the 54 Day Rosary Novena in Gloversville, NY, I told you that there were 3 things that I learned that stood out to me right after I bought my first set of Rosary beads.

> The first thing I learned was the Miraculous 54 Day Rosary Novena.
>
> The second thing I learned was the power of the Rosary and the Scapular working together.
>
> The third thing that I learned and that stood out to me, happened when I was reading Saint Louis De Montfort's excellent book, <u>The Secret of The Rosary.</u> Inside the cover of <u>The Secret of The Rosary</u> there is a quote from the Blessed Mother Mary to Saint Dominic, it reads:

"One day through the Rosary and the Scapular,

I will save the world.[7]

The story of the 54 Day Rosary Novena from Gloversville, NY is one that I wanted to share with you to exhibit events in my and my family's lives that portray special times involving prayer, a sacrament, and strengthened faith.

Today, right now, please make this moment a special time in your own life and begin praying the 54 Day Rosary Novena. Also if the opportunity is present in your area, I highly encourage you to pray the Rosary in the company of Adoration of The Blessed Sacrament.

Blessed Mother Teresa of Calcutta once said, "The time you spend with Jesus in the Blessed Sacrament is the best time you will spend on Earth. Each moment that you spend with Jesus will deepen your union with Him and make your soul everlastingly more glorious and beautiful in Heaven, and will help bring about everlasting peace on Earth."[8]

In 1884, when the Blessed Mother Mary gave to us the 54 Day Rosary Novena, it changed the lives of the Agrelli family in Naples, Italy when they were blessed with miracles for Fortuna's healing. 130 years later it changed the lives of my brother and his wife when they were blessed with miracles during the birth of their three children.

Now is your time to pray the Miraculous 54 Day Rosary Novena.

Through praying the 54 Day Rosary Novena, I hope that in the future it brings you joyful prayer, happiness through the sacraments, strengthened faith, and an abundance of blessings and miracles in your life.

AFTERWORD

The story that you just read originally debuted as a testimonial speech that I gave on June 7, 2015 during the 2nd Anniversary Celebration of Perpetual Eucharistic Adoration at The Church of The Holy Spirit in Gloversville, NY. The day after I gave the speech, I received an e-mail from Gregg Wilbur. I enjoyed reading it, and just wanted to share it with you also.

A copy of Gregg's original e-mail is included below:

June 8, 2015

Hi Chris,

I remember well the night when you went to the adoration chapel to pray for the twins. So glad that God has seen them safely through everything.

Our own story is that when Kim and I got married we prayed that God would bless us with children. We meant one at a time, but didn't actually say that. God answered our prayer almost immediately…and literally…granting us children…our twins. God definitely hears and answers prayer, though in His way, not ours. His way is always better.

Thank you for speaking at yesterday's event. You did a great job.

Gregg Wilbur

THE 15 PROMISES OF MARY TO CHRISTIANS
WHO PRAY THE ROSARY

Made by the Blessed Virgin to St. Dominic and Blessed Alanus.

1. To all those who will recite my Rosary devoutly, I promise my special protection and very great graces.

2. Those who will persevere in the recitation of my Rosary shall receive some signal grace.

3. The Rosary shall be a very powerful armor against hell; it shall destroy vice, deliver from sin, and shall dispel heresy.

4. The Rosary shall make virtue and good works flourish, and shall obtain for souls the most abundant divine mercies; it shall substitute in hearts love of God for love of the world, elevate them to desire heavenly and eternal goods. Oh, that souls would sanctify themselves by this means!

5. "Those who trust themselves to me through the Rosary, shall not perish.

6. Those who will recite my Rosary piously, considering its Mysteries, shall not be overwhelmed by misfortune nor die a bad death. The sinner shall be converted; the just shall grow in grace and become worthy of eternal life.

7. Those truly devoted to my Rosary shall not die without the consolations of the Church, or without grace.

8. Those who will recite my Rosary shall find during their life and at their death the light of God, the fulness of His grace, and shall share in the merits of the blessed.

9. I will deliver very promptly from purgatory the souls devoted to my Rosary.

10. The true children of my Rosary shall enjoy great glory in heaven.

11. *What you ask through my Rosary, you shall obtain.*

12. Those who propagate my Rosary shall obtain through me aid in all their necessities.

13. I have obtained from my Son that all the confreres of the Rosary shall have for their brethren in life and death the saints of Heaven.

14. Those who recite my Rosary faithfully are all my beloved children, the brothers and sisters of Jesus Christ.

15. Devotion to my Rosary is a special sign of predestination.

HOW TO PRAY THE ROSARY

The image on the next page, and the steps below will show you how to pray the Rosary and also display the steps on a set of rosary beads*. These steps are just an overview. They are presented in order, and in more detail for each of the 54 days that follow in the Rosary Novena to Our Lady. The individual prayers for are also written out for you in the pages that follow for the Rosary Novena to Our Lady.

Note: The image of the rosary that shows these steps on rosary beads were used with permission from The Rosary Foundation at www.erosary.com

HOW TO PRAY THE ROSARY STEPS

1. Make the Sign of The Cross and Say The Apostle's Creed.
2. Say one Our Father Prayer.
3. Say three Hail Mary Prayers.
4. Say one Glory Be To The Father Prayer.
5. Say one Fatima Prayer.
6. Announce the First Mystery and Say one Our Father prayer.
7. Say ten consecutive Hail Mary prayers; meditate on the first mystery as you are praying.
8. Say one Glory Be To The Father Prayer.
9. Say one Fatima Prayer.
10. Repeat steps 7, 8, and 9 for the second, third, fourth and fifth mysteries of The Rosary.
11. Say one Hail Holy Queen Prayer.
12. Make The Sign of The Cross

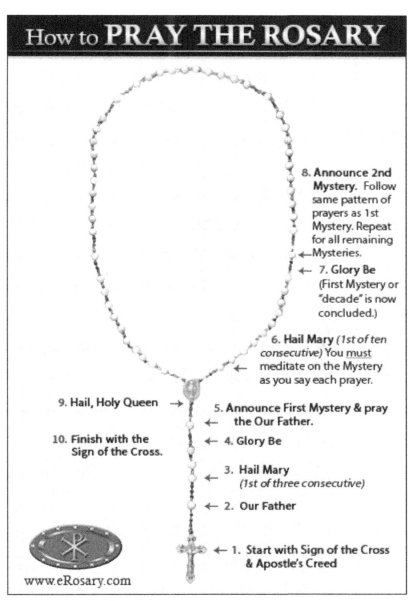

Image Courtesy of Dan Rudden at The Rosary Foundation.

HOW TO REMEMBER WHAT ROSARY DAY YOU'RE ON

One of the challenges in praying the 54 Day Rosary Novena is keeping track of the day and the set of mysteries that you're on.

The two most important things to remember before praying are:

1. Days 1-27 are the prayers in petition for your request.

2. Days 28-54 are the prayers in thanksgiving for your request.

Here are 3 solutions to help you remember what day you're praying:

1. Make a 54 day checklist on a piece of paper and use it as a bookmark inside this book, or keep it aside separately. Check off days after you pray the set of mysteries for the day.

2. When I first started praying the 54 Day Rosary Novena I didn't make a checklist of dates on a piece of paper. Instead I used Excel Spreadsheet to make a calendar of 54 days. A similar example of what my Excel file looked like can be found on page 21. The calendar was 54 days long. After finishing the set of mysteries for the day, I shaded in the box for the day as shown in Day 1. Here the "J" represents the Joyful Mysteries Day. Notice that Day 28 begins the "Thanksgiving" prayers. On day 28 you'll restart the J-L-S-G rotation. If you think this method will work for you, directions to download a free copy of the file can be found at greatpointpublishing.com/store

3. Lastly, probably the easiest way to remember what day you're on is by using the kindle version of this book. It contains all 54 days and all of the individual prayers typed out for you. The electronic bookmark in the e-book will also will help you remember what day you're on after you finish the set of mysteries for the day. The e-book is available at amazon.com Go to amazon and simply search for "54 Day Rosary Novena by Christopher Hallenbeck".

Day 1	Day 2	Day 3	Day 4	Day 5	Day 6
J	L	S	G	J	L
Day 7	Day 8	Day 9	Day 10	Day 11	Day 12
S	G	J	L	S	G
Day 13	Day 14	Day 15	Day 16	Day 17	Day 18
J	L	S	G	J	L
Day 19	Day 20	Day 21	Day 22	Day 23	Day 24
S	G	J	L	S	G
Day 25	Day 26	Day 27	Day 28	Day 29	Day 30
J	L	S	J	L	S

"Example of 54 Day Rosary Novena Calendar using Spreadsheet"

THE MIRACULOUS 54 DAY ROSARY NOVENA TO OUR LADY

THE ROSARY NOVENA
TO OUR LADY

The Joyful Mysteries

Our Lady Of The Holy Rosary Novena Prayer

My dearest Mother Mary, behold me, your child, in prayer at your feet. Accept this Holy Rosary, which I offer you in accordance with your requests at Fatima, as a proof of my tender love for you, for the intentions of the Sacred Heart of Jesus, in atonement for the offenses committed against your Immaculate Heart, and for this special favor which I earnestly request in my Rosary Novena:

(Mention your request).

Please Mother Mary I beg you to present my petition to your Divine Son. If you will pray for me, I cannot be refused. I know, dearest Mother, that you want me to seek God's holy Will concerning my request. If my petition is not compatible with God's Holy Will, and what I ask for should not be granted; please pray that I may receive that which will be the greater benefit to my soul or the person's soul whom I'm praying for.

I offer you this spiritual "Bouquet of Roses" because I love you. I put all my confidence in you, since your prayers before God are most powerful. For the greater glory of God and for the sake of Jesus, your loving Son, hear and grant my prayer. Sweet Heart of Mary, be my salvation.

The Rosary Novena to Our Lady Prayer

In the name of the Father, and the Son, and the Holy Spirit, Amen.

(1) Hail Mary

Hail Mary, full of grace. The Lord is with thee. Blessed art thou amongst women, and blessed is the fruit of thy womb, Jesus. Holy Mary, Mother of God, pray for us sinners, now and at the hour of our death. Amen.

In petition.... (say prayer below when praying during days 1-27.)

Hail, Queen of the Most Holy Rosary, my Mother Mary, hail! At thy feet I humbly kneel to offer thee a Crown of Roses –– snow-white buds to remind thee of thy joys –– each bud recalling to thee a holy mystery; each ten bound together with my petition for a particular grace. O Holy Queen, dispenser of God's graces, and Mother of all who invoke thee! Thou canst not look upon my gift and fail to see its binding. As thou receivest my gift, so wilt thou receive my petition; from thy bounty thou wilt give me the favor I so earnestly and trustingly seek. I despair of nothing that I ask of thee. Show thyself my Mother!

After saying "In Petition Prayer..."" Continue with Rosary Prayers on the next page.

In Thanksgiving.... (say prayer below during days 28-54.)

Hail Queen of the Most Holy Rosary my Mother Mary, Hail! At thy feet I gratefully kneel to offer thee a --Crown of Roses—snow white buds to remind thee of the joys of thy divine Son -- each rose recalling to thee a holy mystery; each ten bound together with my petition for a particular grace. O Holy Queen dispenser of God's graces and Mother of all who invoke thee! Thou canst not look upon my gift and fail to see its binding. As thou receive my gift, so wilt thou receive my thanksgiving; from thy bounty thou hast given me the favor I so earnestly and trustingly sought. I despaired not of what I ask of thee, and thou has truly shown thyself my Mother!

The Apostle's Creed
I believe in God, the Father Almighty, Creator of Heaven and Earth; and in Jesus Christ, His only Son, Our Lord, Who was conceived by the Holy Spirit, born of the Virgin Mary, suffered under Pontius Pilate, was crucified, died, and was buried. He descended into Hell. The third day He arose again from the dead; He ascended into Heaven, sitteth at the right hand of God, the Father Almighty; from thence He shall come to judge the living and the dead. I believe in the Holy Spirit, the holy Catholic Church, the communion of saints, the forgiveness of sins, the resurrection of the body, and the life everlasting. Amen.

(1) Our Father
Our Father, Who art in Heaven, hallowed be Thy name; Thy kingdom come; Thy will be done on Earth as it is in Heaven. Give us this day our daily bread; and forgive us our trespasses as we forgive those who trespass against us; and lead us not into temptation, but deliver us from evil. Amen.

The 3 Hail Mary beads

For an increase in the virtue of faith...I humbly pray:

(1) Hail Mary
Hail Mary, full of grace. The Lord is with thee. Blessed art thou amongst women, and blessed is the fruit of thy womb, Jesus. Holy Mary, Mother of God, pray for us sinners, now and at the hour of our death. Amen.

For an increase in the virtue of hope...I humbly pray:

(1) Hail Mary
Hail Mary, full of grace. The Lord is with thee. Blessed art thou amongst women, and blessed is the fruit of thy womb, Jesus. Holy Mary, Mother of God, pray for us sinners, now and at the hour of our death. Amen.

For an increase in the virtue of charity...I humbly pray:

(1) Hail Mary
Hail Mary, full of grace. The Lord is with thee. Blessed art thou amongst women, and blessed is the fruit of thy womb, Jesus. Holy Mary, Mother of God, pray for us sinners, now and at the hour of our death. Amen.

(1) Glory Be
Glory be to the Father, and to the Son, and to the Holy Spirit, as it was in the beginning, is now, and ever shall be, world without end. Amen.

(1) Oh my Jesus
Oh my Jesus, forgive us our sins, save us from the fires of hell and lead all souls into heaven, especially those in most need of thy mercy. Amen.

THE FIRST JOYFUL MYSTERY

THE ANNUNCIATION

Sweet Mother Mary, meditating on the Mystery of the Annunciation, which we read about in Luke 1:26-38 and John 1:14. When the angel Gabriel appeared to thee with the tidings that thou wert to become the Mother of God, greeting thee with that sublime salutation, "Hail, full of grace! the Lord is with thee!" and thou didst humbly submit thyself to the will of the Father, responding: "Behold the handmaid of the Lord. Be it done unto me according to thy word."

Meditating on the Mystery of The Annunciation and praying for an increase in the virtue of humility…I humbly pray

(1) Our Father

Our Father, Who art in Heaven, hallowed be Thy name; Thy kingdom come; Thy will be done on Earth as it is in Heaven. Give us this day our daily bread; and forgive us our trespasses as we forgive those who trespass against us; and lead us not into temptation, but deliver us from evil. Amen.

(10) Hail Mary

Hail Mary, full of grace. The Lord is with thee. Blessed art thou amongst women, and blessed is the fruit of thy womb, Jesus. Holy Mary, Mother of God, pray for us sinners, now and at the hour of our death. Amen.

(1) Glory Be

Glory be to the Father, and to the Son, and to the Holy Spirit, as it was in the beginning, is now, and ever shall be, world without end. Amen.

(1) Oh my Jesus

Oh my Jesus, forgive us our sins, save us from the fires of hell and lead all souls into heaven, especially those in most need of thy mercy. Amen.

I bind these snow-white buds with a petition for the virtue of

HUMILITY

and humbly lay this bouquet at thy feet.

THE SECOND JOYFUL MYSTERY

THE VISITATION

Sweet Mother Mary, meditating on the Mystery of the Visitation, which we read about in Luke 1:39-56. When, upon thy visit to thy holy cousin Elizabeth, she greeted thee with the prophetic utterance: "Blessed art thou among women, and blessed is the fruit of thy womb!" And thou didst answer with that canticle of canticles, the Magnificat.

Meditating on the Mystery of The Visitation, and praying for an increase in the virtue of charity, I humbly pray...

(1) Our Father

Our Father, Who art in Heaven, hallowed be Thy name; Thy kingdom come; Thy will be done on Earth as it is in Heaven. Give us this day our daily bread; and forgive us our trespasses as we forgive those who trespass against us; and lead us not into temptation, but deliver us from evil. Amen.

(10) Hail Mary

Hail Mary, full of grace. The Lord is with thee. Blessed art thou amongst women, and blessed is the fruit of thy womb, Jesus. Holy Mary, Mother of God, pray for us sinners, now and at the hour of our death. Amen.

(1) Glory Be

Glory be to the Father, and to the Son, and to the Holy Spirit, as it was in the beginning, is now, and ever shall be, world without end. Amen.

(1) Oh my Jesus

Oh my Jesus, forgive us our sins, save us from the fires of hell and lead all souls into heaven, especially those in most need of thy mercy. Amen.

I bind these snow-white buds with a petition for the virtue of

CHARITY

and humbly lay this bouquet at thy feet.

THE THIRD JOYFUL MYSTERY

THE NATIVITY

Sweet Mother Mary, meditating on the Mystery of the Nativity of Our Lord, which we read about in Matthew 1:18-25. When, thy time being completed, thou didst bring forth, O holy Virgin, the Redeemer of the world in a stable at Bethlehem. Whereupon choirs of angels filled the heavens with their exultant song of praise –– "Glory to God in the highest, and on Earth peace to men of good will"

Meditating on the Mystery of The Nativity, and praying for an increase in the virtue of detachment from the world, I humbly pray...

(1) Our Father

Our Father, Who art in Heaven, hallowed be Thy name; Thy kingdom come; Thy will be done on Earth as it is in Heaven. Give us this day our daily bread; and forgive us our trespasses as we forgive those who trespass against us; and lead us not into temptation, but deliver us from evil. Amen.

(10) Hail Mary

Hail Mary, full of grace. The Lord is with thee. Blessed art thou amongst women, and blessed is the fruit of thy womb, Jesus. Holy Mary, Mother of God, pray for us sinners, now and at the hour of our death. Amen.

(1) Glory Be

Glory be to the Father, and to the Son, and to the Holy Spirit, as it was in the beginning, is now, and ever shall be, world without end. Amen.

(1) Oh my Jesus

Oh my Jesus, forgive us our sins, save us from the fires of hell and lead all souls into heaven, especially those in most need of thy mercy. Amen.

I bind these snow-white buds with a petition for the virtue of

DETACHMENT FROM THE WORLD

and humbly lay this bouquet at thy feet.

THE FOURTH JOYFUL MYSTERY

THE PRESENTATION

Sweet Mother Mary, meditating on the Mystery of the Presentation, which we read about in Luke 2:22-39; when, in obedience to the Law of Moses, thou didst present thy Child in the Temple, where the holy prophet Simeon, taking the Child in his arms, offered thanks to God for sparing him to look upon his Savior and foretold thy sufferings by the words: "Thy soul also a sword shall pierce. . ."

Meditating of the Mystery of the Presentation of The Lord, and praying for an increase in the virtue of purity, I humbly pray...

(1) Our Father

Our Father, Who art in Heaven, hallowed be Thy name; Thy kingdom come; Thy will be done on Earth as it is in Heaven. Give us this day our daily bread; and forgive us our trespasses as we forgive those who trespass against us; and lead us not into temptation, but deliver us from evil. Amen.

(10) Hail Mary

Hail Mary, full of grace. The Lord is with thee. Blessed art thou amongst women, and blessed is the fruit of thy womb, Jesus. Holy Mary, Mother of God, pray for us sinners, now and at the hour of our death. Amen.

(1) Glory Be

Glory be to the Father, and to the Son, and to the Holy Spirit, as it was in the beginning, is now, and ever shall be, world without end. Amen.

(1) Oh my Jesus

Oh my Jesus, forgive us our sins, save us from the fires of hell and lead all souls into heaven, especially those in most need of thy mercy. Amen.

I bind these snow-white buds with a petition for the virtue of

PURITY

and humbly lay this bouquet at thy feet.

THE FIFTH JOYFUL MYSTERY

THE FINDING OF THE CHILD JESUS IN THE TEMPLE

Sweet Mother Mary, meditating on the Mystery of the Finding of the Child Jesus in the Temple, which we read about in Luke 2:41-51. When, having sought Him for three days, sorrowing, thy heart was gladdened upon finding Him in the Temple speaking to the doctors. And when, upon thy request, He obediently returned home with thee.

Meditating on the Mystery of The finding of the child Jesus in the Temple, and praying for an increase in the virtue of Obedience to the will of God, I humbly pray...

(1) Our Father
Our Father, Who art in Heaven, hallowed be Thy name; Thy kingdom come; Thy will be done on Earth as it is in Heaven. Give us this day our daily bread; and forgive us our trespasses as we forgive those who trespass against us; and lead us not into temptation, but deliver us from evil. Amen.

(10) Hail Mary
Hail Mary, full of grace. The Lord is with thee. Blessed art thou amongst women, and blessed is the fruit of thy womb, Jesus. Holy Mary, Mother of God, pray for us sinners, now and at the hour of our death. Amen.

(1) Glory Be
Glory be to the Father, and to the Son, and to the Holy Spirit, as it was in the beginning, is now, and ever shall be, world without end. Amen.

(1) Oh my Jesus
Oh my Jesus, forgive us our sins, save us from the fires of hell and lead all souls into heaven, especially those in most need of thy mercy. Amen.

I bind these snow-white buds with a petition for the virtue of

OBEDIENCE TO THE WILL OF GOD

and humbly lay this bouquet at thy feet.

SPIRITUAL COMMUNION

MY JESUS, really present in the most holy Sacrament of the Altar, since I cannot now receive Thee under the sacramental veil, I beseech Thee, with a heart full of love and longing, to come spiritually into my soul through the immaculate heart of Thy most holy Mother, and abide with me forever; Thou in me, and I in Thee, in time and in eternity, in Mary. Amen.

In petition (say when praying days 1-27)

Sweet Mother Mary, I offer thee this Spiritual Communion to bind my bouquets in a wreath to place upon thy brow. O my Mother! look with favor upon my gift, and in thy love obtain for me: *(specify request)* But again only if my request is compatible with God's Holy Will, and if it is for the better of my soul or the person's soul that I'm praying for. For this petition, O Queen of The Holy Rosary, I humbly pray asking for your intercession; *(Hail Mary...Hail Holy Queen...)*

In thanksgiving (say when praying days 28-54)

Sweet Mother Mary, I offer thee this Spiritual Communion to bind my bouquets in a wreath to place upon thy brow in thanksgiving for *(specify request)* which thou in thy love has obtained for me. In thanks Mother Mary, I humbly pray

(1) Hail Mary
Hail Mary, full of grace. The Lord is with thee. Blessed art thou amongst women, and blessed is the fruit of thy womb, Jesus. Holy Mary, Mother of God, pray for us sinners, now and at the hour of our death. Amen.

Hail Holy Queen
Hail, Holy Queen, Mother of mercy, our life, our sweetness and our hope. To thee do we cry, poor banished children of Eve: to thee do we send up our sighs, mourning and weeping in this valley of tears. Turn then, most gracious Advocate, thine eyes of mercy toward us, and

after this our exile, show unto us the blessed fruit of thy womb, Jesus. O clement, O loving, O sweet Virgin Mary! Pray for us, O Holy Mother of God... that we may be made worthy of the promises of Christ. Amen

LET US PRAY
O God! Whose only-begotten Son, by His life, death, and resurrection, has purchased for us the reward of eternal life; grant, we beseech Thee, that, meditating upon these mysteries of the Most Holy Rosary of the Blessed Virgin Mary, we may imitate what they contain and obtain what they promise. Through the same Christ our Lord. Amen.

May the divine assistance remain always with us. Amen. And may the souls of the faithful departed, through the mercy *of* God, rest in peace. Amen. Holy Virgin, with thy loving Child, thy blessing give to us this day *(night)*.

Memorare
Remember, O most gracious Virgin Mary, that never was it known that anyone who fled to thy protection, implored thy help or sought thy intercession, was left unaided. Inspired by this confidence, We fly unto thee, O Virgin of virgins my Mother; to thee do we come, before thee we stand, sinful and sorrowful; O Mother of the Word Incarnate, despise not our petitions, but in thy mercy hear and answer them. Amen.

Saint Michael Prayer
Saint Michael, the Archangel, defend us in battle. Be our protection against the wickedness and snares of the devil. May God rebuke him, we humbly pray; and do thou, O Prince of the heavenly host, by the power of God cast into hell Satan and all the evil spirits who prowl throughout the world seeking the ruin of souls. Amen.

Sign of the Cross
In the name of the Father, and the Son, and the Holy Spirit, Amen.

THE ROSARY NOVENA
TO OUR LADY

The Luminous Mysteries

Our Lady Of The Holy Rosary Novena Prayer

My dearest Mother Mary, behold me, your child, in prayer at your feet. Accept this Holy Rosary, which I offer you in accordance with your requests at Fatima, as a proof of my tender love for you, for the intentions of the Sacred Heart of Jesus, in atonement for the offenses committed against your Immaculate Heart, and for this special favor which I earnestly request in my Rosary Novena:

(Mention your request).

Please Mother Mary I beg you to present my petition to your Divine Son. If you will pray for me, I cannot be refused. I know, dearest Mother, that you want me to seek God's holy Will concerning my request. If my petition is not compatible with God's Holy Will, and what I ask for should not be granted; please pray that I may receive that which will be the greater benefit to my soul or the person's soul whom I'm praying for.

I offer you this spiritual "Bouquet of Roses" because I love you. I put all my confidence in you, since your prayers before God are most powerful. For the greater glory of God and for the sake of Jesus, your loving Son, hear and grant my prayer. Sweet Heart of Mary, be my salvation.

The Rosary Novena to Our Lady Prayer

In the name of the Father, and the Son, and the Holy Spirit, Amen.

(1) Hail Mary

Hail Mary, full of grace. The Lord is with thee. Blessed art thou amongst women, and blessed is the fruit of thy womb, Jesus. Holy Mary, Mother of God, pray for us sinners, now and at the hour of our death. Amen.

In petition.... (say prayer below when praying during days 1-27.)

Hail, Queen of the Most Holy Rosary, my Mother Mary, hail! At thy feet I humbly kneel to offer thee a Crown of Roses –– bright yellow roses to remind thee of thy ministry of your son –– each bud recalling to thee a holy mystery; each ten bound together with my petition for a particular grace. O Holy Queen, dispenser of God's graces, and Mother of all who invoke thee! Thou canst not look upon my gift and fail to see its binding. As thou receivest my gift, so wilt thou receive my petition; from thy bounty thou wilt give me the favor I so earnestly and trustingly seek. I despair of nothing that I ask of thee. Show thyself my Mother!

After saying "In Petition Prayer..."" Continue with Rosary Prayers on the next page.

In Thanksgiving.... (say prayer below during days 28-54.)

Hail Queen of the Most Holy Rosary my Mother Mary, Hail! At thy feet I gratefully kneel to offer thee a --Crown of Roses— bright yellow roses to remind thee of thy ministry of your son --each rose recalling to thee a holy mystery; each ten bound together with my petition for a particular grace. O Holy Queen dispenser of God's graces and Mother of all who invoke thee! Thou canst not look upon my gift and fail to see its binding. As thou receive my gift, so wilt thou receive my thanksgiving; from thy bounty thou hast given me the favor I so earnestly and trustingly sought. I despaired not of what I ask of thee, and thou has truly shown thyself my Mother!

The Apostle's Creed
I believe in God, the Father Almighty, Creator of Heaven and Earth; and in Jesus Christ, His only Son, Our Lord, Who was conceived by the Holy Spirit, born of the Virgin Mary, suffered under Pontius Pilate, was crucified, died, and was buried. He descended into Hell. The third day He arose again from the dead; He ascended into Heaven, sitteth at the right hand of God, the Father Almighty; from thence He shall come to judge the living and the dead. I believe in the Holy Spirit, the holy Catholic Church, the communion of saints, the forgiveness of sins, the resurrection of the body, and the life everlasting. Amen.

(1) Our Father
Our Father, Who art in Heaven, hallowed be Thy name; Thy kingdom come; Thy will be done on Earth as it is in Heaven. Give us this day our daily bread; and forgive us our trespasses as we forgive those who trespass against us; and lead us not into temptation, but deliver us from evil. Amen.

The 3 Hail Mary beads

For an increase in the virtue of faith...I humbly pray:

(1) Hail Mary
Hail Mary, full of grace. The Lord is with thee. Blessed art thou amongst women, and blessed is the fruit of thy womb, Jesus. Holy Mary, Mother of God, pray for us sinners, now and at the hour of our death. Amen.

For an increase in the virtue of hope...I humbly pray:

(1) Hail Mary
Hail Mary, full of grace. The Lord is with thee. Blessed art thou amongst women, and blessed is the fruit of thy womb, Jesus. Holy Mary, Mother of God, pray for us sinners, now and at the hour of our death. Amen.

For an increase in the virtue of charity...I humbly pray:

(1) Hail Mary
Hail Mary, full of grace. The Lord is with thee. Blessed art thou amongst women, and blessed is the fruit of thy womb, Jesus. Holy Mary, Mother of God, pray for us sinners, now and at the hour of our death. Amen.

(1) Glory Be
Glory be to the Father, and to the Son, and to the Holy Spirit, as it was in the beginning, is now, and ever shall be, world without end. Amen.

(1) Oh my Jesus
Oh my Jesus, forgive us our sins, save us from the fires of hell and lead all souls into heaven, especially those in most need of thy mercy. Amen.

THE FIRST MYSTERY OF LIGHT

THE BAPTISM OF JESUS IN THE JORDAN RIVER

O Courageous Mother Mary, meditating on the Mystery of the Baptism of Jesus in the Jordan River which we read about in Matthew 3:11-17; Mark 1:9-11; Luke 3:15-22 and John 1:26-34. When your son, as an example to all, insisted on being baptized by his cousin John and the sky opened and the Holy Spirit came down to him like a dove and a voice from heaven said, "You are my own dear Son in whom I am well pleased."

Meditating on the Baptism of Jesus in the Jordan River and praying for an increase in the virtue of Openness To The Holy Spirit, I humbly pray...

(1) Our Father

Our Father, Who art in Heaven, hallowed be Thy name; Thy kingdom come; Thy will be done on Earth as it is in Heaven. Give us this day our daily bread; and forgive us our trespasses as we forgive those who trespass against us; and lead us not into temptation, but deliver us from evil. Amen.

(10) Hail Mary

Hail Mary, full of grace. The Lord is with thee. Blessed art thou amongst women, and blessed is the fruit of thy womb, Jesus. Holy Mary, Mother of God, pray for us sinners, now and at the hour of our death. Amen.

(1) Glory Be

Glory be to the Father, and to the Son, and to the Holy Spirit, as it was in the beginning, is now, and ever shall be, world without end. Amen.

Oh my Jesus:

Oh my Jesus, forgive us our sins, save us from the fires of hell and lead all souls into heaven, especially those in most need of thy mercy. Amen.

I bind these bright yellow roses with a petition for the virtue of

OPENNESS TO THE HOLY SPIRIT

and humbly lay this bouquet at thy feet.

THE SECOND MYSTERY OF LIGHT

THE WEDDING OF CANA...THE FIRST MIRACLE OF JESUS...

O Courageous Mother Mary, meditating on the Mystery of the First Miracle of Jesus at the Wedding Feast at Cana, the story that we read about in John 2:1-12, when at your urging, your son performed the first of his many miracles by helping a couple celebrate their marriage by changing water into wine of such quality that the chief steward upbraided the host by saying, "Usually people serve the best wine first and save the cheaper wine for last, but you have saved the choice wine for last."

Meditating on the Mystery of The Wedding Feast at Cana, and praying for an increase in the virtue of To Jesus Through Mary, I humbly pray...

(1) Our Father

Our Father, Who art in Heaven, hallowed be Thy name; Thy kingdom come; Thy will be done on Earth as it is in Heaven. Give us this day our daily bread; and forgive us our trespasses as we forgive those who trespass against us; and lead us not into temptation, but deliver us from evil. Amen.

(10) Hail Mary

Hail Mary, full of grace. The Lord is with thee. Blessed art thou amongst women, and blessed is the fruit of thy womb, Jesus. Holy Mary, Mother of God, pray for us sinners, now and at the hour of our death. Amen.

(1) Glory Be

Glory be to the Father, and to the Son, and to the Holy Spirit, as it was in the beginning, is now, and ever shall be, world without end. Amen.

(1) Oh my Jesus:

Oh my Jesus, forgive us our sins, save us from the fires of hell and lead all souls into heaven, especially those in most need of thy mercy. Amen.

I bind these bright yellow roses with a petition for the virtue of

TO JESUS THROUGH MARY

and humbly lay this bouquet at your feet.

THE THIRD MYSTERY OF LIGHT

THE PROCLAMATION OF THE KINGDOM OF GOD

O courageous Mother Mary, meditating on the Mystery of the Proclamation of the Kingdom of God, the story that we read about in Mark 1:14-15, Matthew 5:1-16, Matthew 6:33, and also Matthew 7:21, when your son revealed that the reign of God has already begun "within us" and we are called to conversion and forgiveness, praying "Your Kingdom come, your will be done, on Earth as it is in heaven."

Meditating on the Mystery of the Proclamation of the Kingdom of God, and praying for an increase in the virtue of Repentance and Trust in God, I humbly pray...

(1) Our Father

Our Father, Who art in Heaven, hallowed be Thy name; Thy kingdom come; Thy will be done on Earth as it is in Heaven. Give us this day our daily bread; and forgive us our trespasses as we forgive those who trespass against us; and lead us not into temptation, but deliver us from evil. Amen.

(10) Hail Mary

Hail Mary, full of grace. The Lord is with thee. Blessed art thou amongst women, and blessed is the fruit of thy womb, Jesus. Holy Mary, Mother of God, pray for us sinners, now and at the hour of our death. Amen.

(1) Glory Be

Glory be to the Father, and to the Son, and to the Holy Spirit, as it was in the beginning, is now, and ever shall be, world without end. Amen.

(1) Oh my Jesus:

Oh my Jesus, forgive us our sins, save us from the fires of hell and lead all souls into heaven, especially those in most need of thy mercy. Amen.

I bind these bright yellow roses with a petition for the virtue of

REPENTANCE AND TRUST IN GOD

and humbly lay this bouquet at your feet.

THE FOURTH MYSTERY OF LIGHT

THE TRANSFIGURATION

O courageous Mother Mary, meditating on the Mystery of the Transfiguration, the story that we read about in Matthew 17:1-8, Mark 9:2-10, and Luke 9:28-36, when your son revealed his glory to his three disciples, appearing on a mountain with Moses and Elijah, his face shining like the sun and a voice from heaven proclaiming, "This is my beloved Son...Listen to him."

Meditating on the Mystery of The Transfiguration, and praying for an increase in the virtue of Desire for Holiness, I humbly pray...

(1) Our Father

Our Father, Who art in Heaven, hallowed be Thy name; Thy kingdom come; Thy will be done on Earth as it is in Heaven. Give us this day our daily bread; and forgive us our trespasses as we forgive those who trespass against us; and lead us not into temptation, but deliver us from evil. Amen.

(10) Hail Mary

Hail Mary, full of grace. The Lord is with thee. Blessed art thou amongst women, and blessed is the fruit of thy womb, Jesus. Holy Mary, Mother of God, pray for us sinners, now and at the hour of our death. Amen.

(1) Glory Be

Glory be to the Father, and to the Son, and to the Holy Spirit, as it was in the beginning, is now, and ever shall be, world without end. Amen.

(1) Oh my Jesus:

Oh my Jesus, forgive us our sins, save us from the fires of hell and lead all souls into heaven, especially those in most need of thy mercy. Amen.

I bind these bright yellow roses with a petition for the virtue of

DESIRE FOR HOLINESS

and humbly lay this bouquet at your feet.

THE FIFTH MYSTERY OF LIGHT

THE INSTITUTION OF THE EUCHARIST

O courageous Mother Mary, meditating on the Mystery of the Institution of the Sacrament of the Eucharist, the lesson we are taught in Matthew 26:26-28, Mark 14:22-25, Luke 22:14-20, and John 6:33-59, when on the day before he died, your son celebrated the Passover with his disciples and took bread and gave it to them saying, "Take and eat; this is my body." And when dinner was finished he took a cup of wine and shared it with them saying, "Take and drink; this is my blood, which will be given up for you; do this in memory of me."

Meditating on the Institution of The Eucharist and praying for an increase in the virtue of Adoration of The Eucharist, I humbly pray...

(1) Our Father

Our Father, Who art in Heaven, hallowed be Thy name; Thy kingdom come; Thy will be done on Earth as it is in Heaven. Give us this day our daily bread; and forgive us our trespasses as we forgive those who trespass against us; and lead us not into temptation, but deliver us from evil. Amen.

(10) Hail Mary

Hail Mary, full of grace. The Lord is with thee. Blessed art thou amongst women, and blessed is the fruit of thy womb, Jesus. Holy Mary, Mother of God, pray for us sinners, now and at the hour of our death. Amen.

(1) Glory Be

Glory be to the Father, and to the Son, and to the Holy Spirit, as it was in the beginning, is now, and ever shall be, world without end. Amen.

(1) Oh my Jesus:

Oh my Jesus, forgive us our sins, save us from the fires of hell and lead all souls into heaven, especially those in most need of thy mercy. Amen.

I bind these bright yellow roses with a petition for the virtue of

ADORATION OF THE EUCHARIST

and humbly lay this bouquet at your feet.

SPIRITUAL COMMUNION

MY JESUS, really present in the most holy Sacrament of the Altar, since I cannot now receive Thee under the sacramental veil, I beseech Thee, with a heart full of love and longing, to come spiritually into my soul through the immaculate heart of Thy most holy Mother, and abide with me forever; Thou in me, and I in Thee, in time and in eternity, in Mary. Amen.

In petition (say when praying days 1-27)

Sweet Mother Mary, I offer thee this Spiritual Communion to bind my bouquets in a wreath to place upon thy brow. O my Mother! look with favor upon my gift, and in thy love obtain for me: *(specify request)* But again only if my request is compatible with God's Holy Will, and if it is for the better of my soul or the person's soul that I'm praying for. For this petition, O Queen of The Holy Rosary, I humbly pray asking for your intercession; *(Hail Mary…Hail Holy Queen…)*

In thanksgiving (say when praying days 28-54)

Sweet Mother Mary, I offer thee this Spiritual Communion to bind my bouquets in a wreath to place upon thy brow in thanksgiving for *(specify request)* which thou in thy love has obtained for me. In thanks Mother Mary, I humbly pray

(1) Hail Mary
Hail Mary, full of grace. The Lord is with thee. Blessed art thou amongst women, and blessed is the fruit of thy womb, Jesus. Holy Mary, Mother of God, pray for us sinners, now and at the hour of our death. Amen.

Hail Holy Queen
Hail, Holy Queen, Mother of mercy, our life, our sweetness and our hope. To thee do we cry, poor banished children of Eve: to thee do we send up our sighs, mourning and weeping in this valley of tears. Turn then, most gracious Advocate, thine eyes of mercy toward us, and

after this our exile, show unto us the blessed fruit of thy womb, Jesus. O clement, O loving, O sweet Virgin Mary! Pray for us, O Holy Mother of God... that we may be made worthy of the promises of Christ. Amen

LET US PRAY
O God! Whose only-begotten Son, by His life, death, and resurrection, has purchased for us the reward of eternal life; grant, we beseech Thee, that, meditating upon these mysteries of the Most Holy Rosary of the Blessed Virgin Mary, we may imitate what they contain and obtain what they promise. Through the same Christ our Lord. Amen.

May the divine assistance remain always with us. Amen. And may the souls of the faithful departed, through the mercy *of* God, rest in peace. Amen. Holy Virgin, with thy loving Child, thy blessing give to us this day *(night)*.

Memorare
Remember, O most gracious Virgin Mary, that never was it known that anyone who fled to thy protection, implored thy help or sought thy intercession, was left unaided. Inspired by this confidence, We fly unto thee, O Virgin of virgins my Mother; to thee do we come, before thee we stand, sinful and sorrowful; O Mother of the Word Incarnate, despise not our petitions, but in thy mercy hear and answer them. Amen.

Saint Michael Prayer
Saint Michael, the Archangel, defend us in battle. Be our protection against the wickedness and snares of the devil. May God rebuke him, we humbly pray; and do thou, O Prince of the heavenly host, by the power of God cast into hell Satan and all the evil spirits who prowl throughout the world seeking the ruin of souls. Amen.

Sign of the Cross
In the name of the Father, and the Son, and the Holy Spirit, Amen.

THE ROSARY NOVENA

TO OUR LADY

The Sorrowful Mysteries

Our Lady Of The Holy Rosary Novena Prayer

My dearest Mother Mary, behold me, your child, in prayer at your feet. Accept this Holy Rosary, which I offer you in accordance with your requests at Fatima, as a proof of my tender love for you, for the intentions of the Sacred Heart of Jesus, in atonement for the offenses committed against your Immaculate Heart, and for this special favor which I earnestly request in my Rosary Novena:

(Mention your request).

Please Mother Mary I beg you to present my petition to your Divine Son. If you will pray for me, I cannot be refused. I know, dearest Mother, that you want me to seek God's holy Will concerning my request. If my petition is not compatible with God's Holy Will, and what I ask for should not be granted; please pray that I may receive that which will be the greater benefit to my soul or the person's soul whom I'm praying for.

I offer you this spiritual "Bouquet of Roses" because I love you. I put all my confidence in you, since your prayers before God are most powerful. For the greater glory of God and for the sake of Jesus, your loving Son, hear and grant my prayer. Sweet Heart of Mary, be my salvation.

The Rosary Novena to Our Lady Prayer

In the name of the Father, and the Son, and the Holy Spirit, Amen.

(1) Hail Mary
Hail Mary, full of grace. The Lord is with thee. Blessed art thou amongst women, and blessed is the fruit of thy womb, Jesus. Holy Mary, Mother of God, pray for us sinners, now and at the hour of our death. Amen.

In petition.... (say prayer below when praying during days 1-27.)

Hail, Queen of the Most Holy Rosary, my Mother Mary, hail! At thy feet I humbly kneel to offer thee a Crown of Roses –– blood red roses to remind thee of thy passion of your son –– each bud recalling to thee a holy mystery; each ten bound together with my petition for a particular grace. O Holy Queen, dispenser of God's graces, and Mother of all who invoke thee! Thou canst not look upon my gift and fail to see its binding. As thou receivest my gift, so wilt thou receive my petition; from thy bounty thou wilt give me the favor I so earnestly and trustingly seek. I despair of nothing that I ask of thee. Show thyself my Mother!

After saying "In Petition Prayer..."" Continue with Rosary Prayers on the next page.

In Thanksgiving.... (say prayer below during days 28-54.)

Hail Queen of the Most Holy Rosary my Mother Mary, Hail! At thy feet I gratefully kneel to offer thee a --Crown of Roses— blood red roses to remind thee of thy passion of your son --each rose recalling to thee a holy mystery; each ten bound together with my petition for a particular grace. O Holy Queen dispenser of God's graces and Mother of all who invoke thee! Thou canst not look upon my gift and fail to see its binding. As thou receive my gift, so wilt thou receive my thanksgiving; from thy bounty thou hast given me the favor I so earnestly and trustingly sought. I despaired not of what I ask of thee, and thou has truly shown thyself my Mother!

The Apostle's Creed
I believe in God, the Father Almighty, Creator of Heaven and Earth; and in Jesus Christ, His only Son, Our Lord, Who was conceived by the Holy Spirit, born of the Virgin Mary, suffered under Pontius Pilate, was crucified, died, and was buried. He descended into Hell. The third day He arose again from the dead; He ascended into Heaven, sitteth at the right hand of God, the Father Almighty; from thence He shall come to judge the living and the dead. I believe in the Holy Spirit, the holy Catholic Church, the communion of saints, the forgiveness of sins, the resurrection of the body, and the life everlasting. Amen.

(1) Our Father
Our Father, Who art in Heaven, hallowed be Thy name; Thy kingdom come; Thy will be done on Earth as it is in Heaven. Give us this day our daily bread; and forgive us our trespasses as we forgive those who trespass against us; and lead us not into temptation, but deliver us from evil. Amen.

The 3 Hail Mary beads

For an increase in the virtue of faith...I humbly pray:

(1) Hail Mary
Hail Mary, full of grace. The Lord is with thee. Blessed art thou amongst women, and blessed is the fruit of thy womb, Jesus. Holy Mary, Mother of God, pray for us sinners, now and at the hour of our death. Amen.

For an increase in the virtue of hope...I humbly pray:

(1) Hail Mary
Hail Mary, full of grace. The Lord is with thee. Blessed art thou amongst women, and blessed is the fruit of thy womb, Jesus. Holy Mary, Mother of God, pray for us sinners, now and at the hour of our death. Amen.

For an increase in the virtue of charity...I humbly pray:

(1) Hail Mary
Hail Mary, full of grace. The Lord is with thee. Blessed art thou amongst women, and blessed is the fruit of thy womb, Jesus. Holy Mary, Mother of God, pray for us sinners, now and at the hour of our death. Amen.

(1) Glory Be
Glory be to the Father, and to the Son, and to the Holy Spirit, as it was in the beginning, is now, and ever shall be, world without end. Amen.

(1) Oh my Jesus
Oh my Jesus, forgive us our sins, save us from the fires of hell and lead all souls into heaven, especially those in most need of thy mercy. Amen.

THE FIRST SORROWFUL MYSTERY

THE AGONY IN THE GARDEN

O most sorrowful Mother Mary, meditating on the Mystery of the Agony of Our Lord in the Garden, which we read about in Matthew 26:36-46, Mark 14:32-42, and Luke 22:39-46. When, in the grotto of the Garden of Olives, Jesus saw the sins of the world unfolded before Him by Satan, who sought to dissuade Him from the sacrifice He was about to make. When, His soul shrinking from the sight, and His precious blood flowing from every pore at the vision of the torture and death He was to undergo: thy own sufferings, dear Mother, the future sufferings of His Church, and His own sufferings in the Blessed Sacrament, He cried in anguish, "Abba! Father! if it be possible, let this chalice pass from Me!" But, immediately resigning Himself to His Father's will, He prayed, "Not as I will, but as Thou wilt!"

Meditating on the Mystery of The Agony in the Garden, and praying for an increase in the virtue of Resignation to the Will of God, I humbly pray...

(1) Our Father

Our Father, Who art in Heaven, hallowed be Thy name; Thy kingdom come; Thy will be done on Earth as it is in Heaven. Give us this day our daily bread; and forgive us our trespasses as we forgive those who trespass against us; and lead us not into temptation, but deliver us from evil. Amen.

(10) Hail Mary

Hail Mary, full of grace. The Lord is with thee. Blessed art thou amongst women, and blessed is the fruit of thy womb, Jesus. Holy Mary, Mother of God, pray for us sinners, now and at the hour of our death. Amen.

(1) Glory Be

Glory be to the Father, and to the Son, and to the Holy Spirit, as it was in the beginning, is now, and ever shall be, world without end. Amen.

(1) Oh my Jesus:

Oh my Jesus, forgive us our sins, save us from the fires of hell and lead all souls into heaven, especially those in most need of thy mercy. Amen.

I bind these blood red roses with a petition for the virtue of

RESIGNATION TO THE WILL OF GOD

and humbly lay this bouquet at your feet.

THE SECOND SORROWFUL MYSTERY

THE SCOURGING AT THE PILLAR

O most sorrowful Mother Mary, meditating on the Mystery of the Scourging of Our Lord, which we read about in Matthew 27:26, Mark 15:15, Luke 23:16-22, and John 19:1. When, at Pilate's command, thy divine Son, stripped of His garments and bound to a pillar, was lacerated from head to foot with cruel scourges and His flesh torn away until His mortified body could bear no more.

Meditating on the Mystery of the Scourging at the Pillar and praying for an increase in the virtue of Mortification, I humbly pray...

(1) Our Father

Our Father, Who art in Heaven, hallowed be Thy name; Thy kingdom come; Thy will be done on Earth as it is in Heaven. Give us this day our daily bread; and forgive us our trespasses as we forgive those who trespass against us; and lead us not into temptation, but deliver us from evil. Amen.

(10) Hail Mary

Hail Mary, full of grace. The Lord is with thee. Blessed art thou amongst women, and blessed is the fruit of thy womb, Jesus. Holy Mary, Mother of God, pray for us sinners, now and at the hour of our death. Amen.

(1) Glory Be

Glory be to the Father, and to the Son, and to the Holy Spirit, as it was in the beginning, is now, and ever shall be, world without end. Amen.

(1) Oh my Jesus:

Oh my Jesus, forgive us our sins, save us from the fires of hell and lead all souls into heaven, especially those in most need of thy mercy. Amen.

I bind these blood red roses with a petition for the virtue of

MORTIFICATION

and humbly lay this bouquet at your feet.

THE THIRD SORROWFUL MYSTERY

THE CROWNING WITH THORNS

O most sorrowful Mother Mary, meditating, on the Mystery of the Crowning of Our Lord with thorns, which we read about in Matthew 27:29-30, Mark 15:16-20, and John 19: 2-3. When, the soldiers, binding about His head a crown of sharp thorns, showered blows upon it, driving the thorns deeply into His head. When they then, in mock adoration, knelt before Him, crying, "Hail, King of the Jews!'

Meditating on the Mystery of The Crowning of Thorns and praying for an increase in the virtue of humility, I humbly pray...

(1) Our Father

Our Father, Who art in Heaven, hallowed be Thy name; Thy kingdom come; Thy will be done on Earth as it is in Heaven. Give us this day our daily bread; and forgive us our trespasses as we forgive those who trespass against us; and lead us not into temptation, but deliver us from evil. Amen.

(10) Hail Mary

Hail Mary, full of grace. The Lord is with thee. Blessed art thou amongst women, and blessed is the fruit of thy womb, Jesus. Holy Mary, Mother of God, pray for us sinners, now and at the hour of our death. Amen.

(1) Glory Be

Glory be to the Father, and to the Son, and to the Holy Spirit, as it was in the beginning, is now, and ever shall be, world without end. Amen.

(1) Oh my Jesus:

Oh my Jesus, forgive us our sins, save us from the fires of hell and lead all souls into heaven, especially those in most need of thy mercy. Amen.

I bind these blood red roses with a petition for the virtue of

HUMILITY

and humbly lay this bouquet at your feet.

THE FOURTH SORROWFUL MYSTERY

THE CARRYING OF THE CROSS

O most sorrowful Mother Mary, meditating on the Mystery of the Carrying of the Cross, which we read about in Luke 23: 26-32, Matthew 27:31-32, Mark 15:21, and John 19:17. When, with the heavy wood of the cross upon His shoulders, thy divine Son was dragged, weak and suffering, yet patient, through the streets amidst the revilements of the people to Calvary, falling often, but urged along by the cruel blows of His executioners.

Meditating on the Mystery of the Carrying of The Cross, and praying for an increase in the virtue of Patience in Adversity, I humbly pray...

(1) Our Father

Our Father, Who art in Heaven, hallowed be Thy name; Thy kingdom come; Thy will be done on Earth as it is in Heaven. Give us this day our daily bread; and forgive us our trespasses as we forgive those who trespass against us; and lead us not into temptation, but deliver us from evil. Amen.

(10) Hail Mary

Hail Mary, full of grace. The Lord is with thee. Blessed art thou amongst women, and blessed is the fruit of thy womb, Jesus. Holy Mary, Mother of God, pray for us sinners, now and at the hour of our death. Amen.

(1) Glory Be

Glory be to the Father, and to the Son, and to the Holy Spirit, as it was in the beginning, is now, and ever shall be, world without end. Amen.

(1) Oh my Jesus:

Oh my Jesus, forgive us our sins, save us from the fires of hell and lead all souls into heaven, especially those in most need of thy mercy. Amen.

I bind these blood red roses with a petition for the virtue of

PATIENCE IN ADVERSITY

and humbly lay this bouquet at your feet.

THE FIFTH SORROWFUL MYSTERY

THE CRUCIFIXION

O most Sorrowful Mother Mary, meditating on the Mystery of the Crucifixion, which we read about in Luke 23: 33-49; Matthew 27: 33-54; Mark 15: 22-39; and John 19: 17-37; when having been stripped of His garments, thy divine Son was nailed to the cross, upon which He died after three hours of indescribable agony, during which time He begged from His Father forgiveness for His enemies.

Meditating on the Mystery of the Crucifixion, and praying for an increase in the virtue of Love of our Enemies, I humbly pray...

(1) Our Father

Our Father, Who art in Heaven, hallowed be Thy name; Thy kingdom come; Thy will be done on Earth as it is in Heaven. Give us this day our daily bread; and forgive us our trespasses as we forgive those who trespass against us; and lead us not into temptation, but deliver us from evil. Amen.

(10) Hail Mary

Hail Mary, full of grace. The Lord is with thee. Blessed art thou amongst women, and blessed is the fruit of thy womb, Jesus. Holy Mary, Mother of God, pray for us sinners, now and at the hour of our death. Amen.

(1) Glory Be

Glory be to the Father, and to the Son, and to the Holy Spirit, as it was in the beginning, is now, and ever shall be, world without end. Amen.

(1) Oh my Jesus:

Oh my Jesus, forgive us our sins, save us from the fires of hell and lead all souls into heaven, especially those in most need of thy mercy. Amen.

I bind these blood red roses with a petition for the virtue of

LOVE OF OUR ENEMIES

and humbly lay this bouquet at your feet.

SPIRITUAL COMMUNION

MY JESUS, really present in the most holy Sacrament of the Altar, since I cannot now receive Thee under the sacramental veil, I beseech Thee, with a heart full of love and longing, to come spiritually into my soul through the immaculate heart of Thy most holy Mother, and abide with me forever; Thou in me, and I in Thee, in time and in eternity, in Mary. Amen.

In petition (say when praying days 1-27)

Sweet Mother Mary, I offer thee this Spiritual Communion to bind my bouquets in a wreath to place upon thy brow. O my Mother! look with favor upon my gift, and in thy love obtain for me: *(specify request)* But again only if my request is compatible with God's Holy Will, and if it is for the better of my soul or the person's soul that I'm praying for. For this petition, O Queen of The Holy Rosary, I humbly pray asking for your intercession; *(Hail Mary...Hail Holy Queen...)*

In thanksgiving (say when praying days 28-54)

Sweet Mother Mary, I offer thee this Spiritual Communion to bind my bouquets in a wreath to place upon thy brow in thanksgiving for *(specify request)* which thou in thy love has obtained for me. In thanks Mother Mary, I humbly pray

(1) Hail Mary
Hail Mary, full of grace. The Lord is with thee. Blessed art thou amongst women, and blessed is the fruit of thy womb, Jesus. Holy Mary, Mother of God, pray for us sinners, now and at the hour of our death. Amen.

Hail Holy Queen
Hail, Holy Queen, Mother of mercy, our life, our sweetness and our hope. To thee do we cry, poor banished children of Eve: to thee do we send up our sighs, mourning and weeping in this valley of tears. Turn then, most gracious Advocate, thine eyes of mercy toward us, and

after this our exile, show unto us the blessed fruit of thy womb, Jesus. O clement, O loving, O sweet Virgin Mary! Pray for us, O Holy Mother of God... that we may be made worthy of the promises of Christ. Amen

LET US PRAY
O God! Whose only-begotten Son, by His life, death, and resurrection, has purchased for us the reward of eternal life; grant, we beseech Thee, that, meditating upon these mysteries of the Most Holy Rosary of the Blessed Virgin Mary, we may imitate what they contain and obtain what they promise. Through the same Christ our Lord. Amen.

May the divine assistance remain always with us. Amen. And may the souls of the faithful departed, through the mercy of God, rest in peace. Amen. Holy Virgin, with thy loving Child, thy blessing give to us this day *(night)*.

Memorare
Remember, O most gracious Virgin Mary, that never was it known that anyone who fled to thy protection, implored thy help or sought thy intercession, was left unaided. Inspired by this confidence, We fly unto thee, O Virgin of virgins my Mother; to thee do we come, before thee we stand, sinful and sorrowful; O Mother of the Word Incarnate, despise not our petitions, but in thy mercy hear and answer them. Amen.

Saint Michael Prayer
Saint Michael, the Archangel, defend us in battle. Be our protection against the wickedness and snares of the devil. May God rebuke him, we humbly pray; and do thou, O Prince of the heavenly host, by the power of God cast into hell Satan and all the evil spirits who prowl throughout the world seeking the ruin of souls. Amen.

Sign of the Cross
In the name of the Father, and the Son, and the Holy Spirit, Amen.

THE ROSARY NOVENA TO OUR LADY

Photo Courtesy of: Esther Gefroh

The Glorious Mysteries

Our Lady Of The Holy Rosary Novena Prayer

My dearest Mother Mary, behold me, your child, in prayer at your feet. Accept this Holy Rosary, which I offer you in accordance with your requests at Fatima, as a proof of my tender love for you, for the intentions of the Sacred Heart of Jesus, in atonement for the offenses committed against your Immaculate Heart, and for this special favor which I earnestly request in my Rosary Novena:

(Mention your request).

Please Mother Mary I beg you to present my petition to your Divine Son. If you will pray for me, I cannot be refused. I know, dearest Mother, that you want me to seek God's holy Will concerning my request. If my petition is not compatible with God's Holy Will, and what I ask for should not be granted; please pray that I may receive that which will be the greater benefit to my soul or the person's soul whom I'm praying for.

I offer you this spiritual "Bouquet of Roses" because I love you. I put all my confidence in you, since your prayers before God are most powerful. For the greater glory of God and for the sake of Jesus, your loving Son, hear and grant my prayer. Sweet Heart of Mary, be my salvation.

The Rosary Novena to Our Lady Prayer

In the name of the Father, and the Son, and the Holy Spirit, Amen.

(1) Hail Mary

Hail Mary, full of grace. The Lord is with thee. Blessed art thou amongst women, and blessed is the fruit of thy womb, Jesus. Holy Mary, Mother of God, pray for us sinners, now and at the hour of our death. Amen.

In petition.... (say prayer below when praying during days 1-27.)

Hail, Queen of the Most Holy Rosary, my Mother Mary, hail! At thy feet I humbly kneel to offer thee a Crown of Roses –– full blown white roses, tinged with red of the passion, with a glow of yellow light to remind thee of the glories, fruits and sufferings of thy Son and thee –– each bud recalling to thee a holy mystery; each ten bound together with my petition for a particular grace. O Holy Queen, dispenser of God's graces, and Mother of all who invoke thee! Thou canst not look upon my gift and fail to see its binding. As thou receivest my gift, so wilt thou receive my petition; from thy bounty thou wilt give me the favor I so earnestly and trustingly seek. I despair of nothing that I ask of thee. Show thyself my Mother!

After saying "In Petition Prayer..."" Continue with Rosary Prayers on the next page.

In Thanksgiving.... (say prayer below during days 28-54.)

Hail Queen of the Most Holy Rosary my Mother Mary, Hail! At thy feet I gratefully kneel to offer thee a --Crown of Roses— full blown white roses, tinged with red of the passion, with a glow of yellow light to remind thee of the glories, fruits and sufferings of thy Son and thee --each rose recalling to thee a holy mystery; each ten bound together with my petition for a particular grace. O Holy Queen dispenser of God's graces and Mother of all who invoke thee! Thou canst not look upon my gift and fail to see its binding. As thou receive my gift, so wilt thou receive my thanksgiving; from thy bounty thou hast given me the favor I so earnestly and trustingly sought. I despaired not of what I ask of thee, and thou has truly shown thyself my Mother!

The Apostle's Creed
I believe in God, the Father Almighty, Creator of Heaven and Earth; and in Jesus Christ, His only Son, Our Lord, Who was conceived by the Holy Spirit, born of the Virgin Mary, suffered under Pontius Pilate, was crucified, died, and was buried. He descended into Hell. The third day He arose again from the dead; He ascended into Heaven, sitteth at the right hand of God, the Father Almighty; from thence He shall come to judge the living and the dead. I believe in the Holy Spirit, the holy Catholic Church, the communion of saints, the forgiveness of sins, the resurrection of the body, and the life everlasting. Amen.

(1) Our Father
Our Father, Who art in Heaven, hallowed be Thy name; Thy kingdom come; Thy will be done on Earth as it is in Heaven. Give us this day our daily bread; and forgive us our trespasses as we forgive those who trespass against us; and lead us not into temptation, but deliver us from evil. Amen.

The 3 Hail Mary beads

For an increase in the virtue of faith...I humbly pray:

(1) Hail Mary
Hail Mary, full of grace. The Lord is with thee. Blessed art thou amongst women, and blessed is the fruit of thy womb, Jesus. Holy Mary, Mother of God, pray for us sinners, now and at the hour of our death. Amen.

For an increase in the virtue of hope...I humbly pray:

(1) Hail Mary
Hail Mary, full of grace. The Lord is with thee. Blessed art thou amongst women, and blessed is the fruit of thy womb, Jesus. Holy Mary, Mother of God, pray for us sinners, now and at the hour of our death. Amen.

For an increase in the virtue of charity...I humbly pray:

(1) Hail Mary
Hail Mary, full of grace. The Lord is with thee. Blessed art thou amongst women, and blessed is the fruit of thy womb, Jesus. Holy Mary, Mother of God, pray for us sinners, now and at the hour of our death. Amen.

(1) Glory Be
Glory be to the Father, and to the Son, and to the Holy Spirit, as it was in the beginning, is now, and ever shall be, world without end. Amen.

(1) Oh my Jesus
Oh my Jesus, forgive us our sins, save us from the fires of hell and lead all souls into heaven, especially those in most need of thy mercy. Amen.

THE FIRST GLORIOUS MYSTERY

THE RESURRECTION

O glorious Mother Mary, meditating on the Mystery of the Resurrection of Our Lord from the Dead, which we read in Matthew 28: 1-10; Mark 16: 1-18; Luke 24: 1-49; and John 20:1-29, when on the morning of the third day after His death and burial, Jesus arose from the dead and appeared to thee, Blessed Mother, and filled thy heart with unspeakable joy; then appeared to the holy women, and to His disciples, who adored Him as their risen God.

Meditating on Mystery of the Resurrection of Our Lord from the Dead and praying for an increase in the virtue of Faith I humbly pray...

(1) Our Father

Our Father, Who art in Heaven, hallowed be Thy name; Thy kingdom come; Thy will be done on Earth as it is in Heaven. Give us this day our daily bread; and forgive us our trespasses as we forgive those who trespass against us; and lead us not into temptation, but deliver us from evil. Amen.

(10) Hail Mary

Hail Mary, full of grace. The Lord is with thee. Blessed art thou amongst women, and blessed is the fruit of thy womb, Jesus. Holy Mary, Mother of God, pray for us sinners, now and at the hour of our death. Amen.

(1) Glory Be

Glory be to the Father, and to the Son, and to the Holy Spirit, as it was in the beginning, is now, and ever shall be, world without end. Amen.

(1) Oh my Jesus:

Oh my Jesus, forgive us our sins, save us from the fires of hell and lead all souls into heaven, especially those in most need of thy mercy. Amen.

I bind these full blown roses with a petition for the virtue of

FAITH

and humbly lay this bouquet at your feet.

THE SECOND GLORIOUS MYSTERY

THE ASCENSION

O glorious Mother Mary, meditating on the Mystery of the Ascension, which we read in Mark: 16: 19-20; Luke 24: 50-51; and Acts 1: 6-11, when thy divine Son, after forty days on Earth, went to Mount Olivet accompanied by His disciples and thee, where all adored Him for the last time, after which He promised to remain with them until the end of the world; then, extending His pierced hands over all in a last blessing, as ascended before their eyes into heaven.

Meditating on Mystery of the Ascension of Our Lord and praying for an increase in the virtue of Hope...I humbly pray...

(1) Our Father

Our Father, Who art in Heaven, hallowed be Thy name; Thy kingdom come; Thy will be done on Earth as it is in Heaven. Give us this day our daily bread; and forgive us our trespasses as we forgive those who trespass against us; and lead us not into temptation, but deliver us from evil. Amen.

(10) Hail Mary

Hail Mary, full of grace. The Lord is with thee. Blessed art thou amongst women, and blessed is the fruit of thy womb, Jesus. Holy Mary, Mother of God, pray for us sinners, now and at the hour of our death. Amen.

(1) Glory Be

Glory be to the Father, and to the Son, and to the Holy Spirit, as it was in the beginning, is now, and ever shall be, world without end. Amen.

(1) Oh my Jesus:

Oh my Jesus, forgive us our sins, save us from the fires of hell and lead all souls into heaven, especially those in most need of thy mercy. Amen.

I bind these full blown roses with a petition for the virtue of

HOPE

and humbly lay this bouquet at your feet.

THE THIRD GLORIOUS MYSTERY

THE DESCENT OF THE HOLY SPIRIT

O glorious Mother Mary, meditating on the Mystery of the Descent of the Holy Ghost, which we read Acts 2:1-41 when the apostles being assembled with thee in a house in Jerusalem, the Holy Spirit descended upon them in the form of fiery tongues, inflaming the hearts of the apostles with the fire of divine love, teaching them all truths, giving to them the gift of tongues, and, filling thee with the plenitude of His grace, inspired thee to pray for the apostles and the first Christians.

Meditating on Mystery of the descent of The Holy Spirit of Our Lord and praying for an increase in the virtue of Charity...I humbly pray...

(1) Our Father

Our Father, Who art in Heaven, hallowed be Thy name; Thy kingdom come; Thy will be done on Earth as it is in Heaven. Give us this day our daily bread; and forgive us our trespasses as we forgive those who trespass against us; and lead us not into temptation, but deliver us from evil. Amen.

(10) Hail Mary

Hail Mary, full of grace. The Lord is with thee. Blessed art thou amongst women, and blessed is the fruit of thy womb, Jesus. Holy Mary, Mother of God, pray for us sinners, now and at the hour of our death. Amen.

(1) Glory Be

Glory be to the Father, and to the Son, and to the Holy Spirit, as it was in the beginning, is now, and ever shall be, world without end. Amen.

(1) Oh my Jesus:

Oh my Jesus, forgive us our sins, save us from the fires of hell and lead all souls into heaven, especially those in most need of thy mercy. Amen.

I bind these full blown roses with a petition for the virtue of

CHARITY

and humbly lay this bouquet at your feet.

THE FOURTH GLORIOUS MYSTERY

THE ASSUMPTION OF OUR BLESSED MOTHER INTO HEAVEN

O glorious Mother Mary, meditating on the Mystery of Thy Assumption into Heaven, when consumed with the desire to be united with thy divine Son in heaven, thy soul departed from thy body and united itself to Him, Who, out of the excessive love He bore for thee, His Mother, whose virginal body was His first tabernacle, took that body into heaven and there, amidst the acclaims of the angels and saints, reinfused into it thy soul. Meditating on Mystery of The Assumption of Our Blessed Mother into Heaven, which is implied in the book of Revelation 12:1, is taught in The Catechism of the Catholic Church when the Assumption is defined in Sections 966 and 974, and lastly The Assumption is a part of Catholic Tradition...

Meditating on Mystery of The Assumption of Our Blessed Mother into Heaven and praying for an increase in the virtue of Union with Christ...I humbly pray...

(1) Our Father

Our Father, Who art in Heaven, hallowed be Thy name; Thy kingdom come; Thy will be done on Earth as it is in Heaven. Give us this day our daily bread; and forgive us our trespasses as we forgive those who trespass against us; and lead us not into temptation, but deliver us from evil. Amen.

(10) Hail Mary

Hail Mary, full of grace. The Lord is with thee. Blessed art thou amongst women, and blessed is the fruit of thy womb, Jesus. Holy Mary, Mother of God, pray for us sinners, now and at the hour of our death. Amen.

(1) Glory Be

Glory be to the Father, and to the Son, and to the Holy Spirit, as it was in the beginning, is now, and ever shall be, world without end. Amen.

(1) Oh my Jesus:

Oh my Jesus, forgive us our sins, save us from the fires of hell and lead all souls into heaven, especially those in most need of thy mercy. Amen.

I bind these full blown roses with a petition for the virtue of

UNION WITH CHRIST

and humbly lay this bouquet at your feet.

THE FIFTH GLORIOUS MYSTERY

*THE CORONATION OF OUR BLESSED MOTHER
IN HEAVEN AS ITS QUEEN*

O glorious Mother Mary, meditating on the Mystery of Thy Coronation in Heaven which is implied in the book of Revelation 12:1, and also celebrated annually on August 22nd when Catholics celebrate the feast of the Queenship of Mary. O Queen of The Holy Rosary, when upon being taken up to Heaven after thy death, thou wert triply crowned as the August Queen of Heaven. First by God the Father as His beloved Daughter, next by God the Son as His dearest Mother, and finally by God the Holy Ghost as His chaste Spouse, the most perfect adorer of the Blessed Trinity, pleading our cause as our most powerful and merciful Mother.

Meditating on Mystery of The Coronation of Our Blessed Mother in Heaven as its Queen, and praying for an increase in the virtue of Union with Thee, I humbly pray...

(1) Our Father

Our Father, Who art in Heaven, hallowed be Thy name; Thy kingdom come; Thy will be done on Earth as it is in Heaven. Give us this day our daily bread; and forgive us our trespasses as we forgive those who trespass against us; and lead us not into temptation, but deliver us from evil. Amen.

(10) Hail Mary

Hail Mary, full of grace. The Lord is with thee. Blessed art thou amongst women, and blessed is the fruit of thy womb, Jesus. Holy Mary, Mother of God, pray for us sinners, now and at the hour of our death. Amen.

(1) Glory Be

Glory be to the Father, and to the Son, and to the Holy Spirit, as it was in the beginning, is now, and ever shall be, world without end. Amen.

(1) Oh my Jesus:

Oh my Jesus, forgive us our sins, save us from the fires of hell and lead all souls into heaven, especially those in most need of thy mercy. Amen.

I bind these full blown roses with a petition for the virtue of

UNION WITH THEE

and humbly lay this bouquet at your feet.

SPIRITUAL COMMUNION

MY JESUS, really present in the most holy Sacrament of the Altar, since I cannot now receive Thee under the sacramental veil, I beseech Thee, with a heart full of love and longing, to come spiritually into my soul through the immaculate heart of Thy most holy Mother, and abide with me forever; Thou in me, and I in Thee, in time and in eternity, in Mary. Amen.

In petition (say when praying days 1-27)

Sweet Mother Mary, I offer thee this Spiritual Communion to bind my bouquets in a wreath to place upon thy brow. O my Mother! look with favor upon my gift, and in thy love obtain for me: *(specify request)* But again only if my request is compatible with God's Holy Will, and if it is for the better of my soul or the person's soul that I'm praying for. For this petition, O Queen of The Holy Rosary, I humbly pray asking for your intercession; *(Hail Mary...Hail Holy Queen...)*

In thanksgiving (say when praying days 28-54)

Sweet Mother Mary, I offer thee this Spiritual Communion to bind my bouquets in a wreath to place upon thy brow in thanksgiving for *(specify request)* which thou in thy love has obtained for me. In thanks Mother Mary, I humbly pray

(1) Hail Mary
Hail Mary, full of grace. The Lord is with thee. Blessed art thou amongst women, and blessed is the fruit of thy womb, Jesus. Holy Mary, Mother of God, pray for us sinners, now and at the hour of our death. Amen.

Hail Holy Queen
Hail, Holy Queen, Mother of mercy, our life, our sweetness and our hope. To thee do we cry, poor banished children of Eve: to thee do we send up our sighs, mourning and weeping in this valley of tears. Turn then, most gracious Advocate, thine eyes of mercy toward us, and

after this our exile, show unto us the blessed fruit of thy womb, Jesus. O clement, O loving, O sweet Virgin Mary! Pray for us, O Holy Mother of God... that we may be made worthy of the promises of Christ. Amen

LET US PRAY
O God! Whose only-begotten Son, by His life, death, and resurrection, has purchased for us the reward of eternal life; grant, we beseech Thee, that, meditating upon these mysteries of the Most Holy Rosary of the Blessed Virgin Mary, we may imitate what they contain and obtain what they promise. Through the same Christ our Lord. Amen.

May the divine assistance remain always with us. Amen. And may the souls of the faithful departed, through the mercy *of* God, rest in peace. Amen. Holy Virgin, with thy loving Child, thy blessing give to us this day *(night)*.

Memorare
Remember, O most gracious Virgin Mary, that never was it known that anyone who fled to thy protection, implored thy help or sought thy intercession, was left unaided. Inspired by this confidence, We fly unto thee, O Virgin of virgins my Mother; to thee do we come, before thee we stand, sinful and sorrowful; O Mother of the Word Incarnate, despise not our petitions, but in thy mercy hear and answer them. Amen.

Saint Michael Prayer
Saint Michael, the Archangel, defend us in battle. Be our protection against the wickedness and snares of the devil. May God rebuke him, we humbly pray; and do thou, O Prince of the heavenly host, by the power of God cast into hell Satan and all the evil spirits who prowl throughout the world seeking the ruin of souls. Amen.

Sign of the Cross
In the name of the Father, and the Son, and the Holy Spirit, Amen.

About The Author

Christopher Hallenbeck is a 4th Degree Sir Knight in Saint René Goupil Assembly #1427, and a 3rd Degree Brother Knight in Knights of Columbus Council #265 located in Gloversville, NY. Chris is a 10 time Past Grand Knight of Council 265, and also a Past Faithful Navigator of Assembly #1427. During the time he served as Grand Knight, Council 265 earned many awards in recognition of their service to the Catholic Church, the community, and also to The Order. In March 2018 Chris was asked to be a Knights of Columbus Membership Coordinator for The Capital Conference in New York State. In this role he developed and introduced to The Knights of Columbus his well-received presentation entitled "117 Personal Recruiting Strategies to Revitalize Your Council." To learn more about the Knights of Columbus visit *gloversvillekofc.org* or *kofc.org*

Thanks and Acknowledgments

Thank you Mom, Mike, Kolin, Diana and Abbey. Olivia, Luciana, Connor, Jackson, and Finley. Brian Brown. Mary Jo and Cubby Faville. Kelli, Jamie, Melissa and families. Knights of Columbus Council #265. Bishop Ed Scharfenberger. Father Don Czelusniak. Father Rendell Torres. Father Matthew Wetsel. Father James Davis. Father Francis Vivacqua. Father David LeFort. Father Donald Rutherford. Diane Sgroi. Charles V. Lacey. The Adorers at the Perpetual Eucharistic Adoration Chapel at The Church of The Holy Spirit in Gloversville. Diana Hallenbeck, Melissa Faville Hally, Dr. Lana Mowdy, and Maren Kate Ruth for your proofreading and editing help. Esther Gefroh, owner of blogspot "A Catholic Mom in Hawaii" for permission to use her photo of the Our Lady of Fatima Statue. Dan Rudden, owner and operator of The Rosary Foundation, for permission to use the How to Pray The Rosary image. Last but not least, I'd especially like to thank vocalist Francesca Bergamini for sending me music. Your songs were a part of the playlist that I listened to while I worked on writing this book.

Thank You for praying the Rosary.

About Salvatore "Sam" Guarnier

By: Christopher Hallenbeck

Eulogy written on November 6, 2006 and read the next day during Sam's Funeral Mass.

Salvatore "Sam" Guarnier
Gloversville, NY

Salvatore Angelo Guarnier meant a lot of different things to a lot of different people. He was a son, a brother, a husband, a father, an uncle, a Grandfather, a handball partner, a brother of the Knights of Columbus, a member of the YMCA, and a friend to many different people and to many different lives; most importantly though, Grandpa Sam was a role model.

Earlier this year Grandpa celebrated his 90th birthday, and to commemorate the occasion we had a party that included a big cake. This cake was big not because we needed one that could hold 90 candles, we needed a cake big enough that would ensure that everyone in the room would get a piece.

Not many people are fortunate enough to have a 90th birthday party, yet alone to have lived a life so full where the invitation list had to be narrowed down simply because there wasn't enough room for everyone to attend...To all of these people, and to many others who passed away prior, Grandpa Sam was well liked, well respected, and he was in some form or another admired as a role model.

That day after dinner basically everyone in the room stood and spoke of Grandpa with high regards, respect and appreciation for the type of man he was and type of devotion, dedication, and love that he had for his community, his church, his friends, and most importantly his family.

As you all are well aware Grandpa lived each day to its fullest, whether he was volunteering his time for the Knights of Columbus, playing handball with Guy, Art Frank, and Marshall, helping Judge DeSantis campaign for election- and then asking him for his autograph after he won, driving the Fulton County Sheriff and his buddies to Yankee Stadium, running his daily 3 miles at the Darling Field track, or just keeping boxscores of the Yankee Games on TV, Grandpa lived everyday with a smile on his face. However nothing put a bigger smile on his face though than time spent with his family.

To him everyday living that involved his family wasn't an ordinary day, it was a holiday. Grandpa loved his family and enjoyed their company more than anything else. Whether it was a big family get together or the regular phone calls he received from his Daughters, his son, or his grandchildren. Grandpa loved nothing more then spending time with his family. These were the times that he cherished most, and to his family these were times that we spent with the best role model that all of us will ever know.

As we celebrate Grandpa Sam's life today, please remember our Grandpa not just for the times that you spent together with him; remember him for the type of person he was and how he influenced your life through his devotion, dedication, love and respect. Through these thoughts and memories of Grandpa, we all are given the opportunity to show our own individual communities, churches, friends, and families the same devotion, dedication, love and respect that he influenced on us; and hopefully we can all make the world a better place to live simply because Salvatore Angelo Guarnier was a role model to you.

On behalf of my family I'd like to extend an invitation to all of you to join us at the end of this morning's services for a reception at the Knights of Columbus Council 265, 99 North Main Street in Gloversville. Thank You.

About Margaret Guarnier

By: Christopher Hallenbeck

Eulogy written on August 22, 2011, and read the next day during Margaret's Funeral Mass.

Margaret Guarnier with "Marley".
Gloversville, NY

Margaret Peters Guarnier meant a lot of different things to a lot of different people. She was a daughter, a sister, a wife, a mother, an aunt, a grandmother, and a friend to many different people and to many different lives.

In the days since Grandma has passed away, my family has received many phone calls, cards, and messages from friends, and members in the community who have contacted us wanting to express their condolences and offer their support. One of the cards that we received was from my Godparents- Kevin and Ruth Santabarbara who live in Rotterdam, NY and I would like to share it with you. It reads:

"Thinking of you as you honor your Mother:

You'll never forget your mother's face, the sound of her voice, the gentleness of her touch...they let you know you were loved.

You'll never forget the stories she told, the traditions she handed down...they let you know who you are.

You'll never forget the lessons she taught, the things she stood for...they are her gift and your legacy.

You'll never forget, and you'll always know, that you honor her everyday in how you live and who you are."

When I first greeted you today with my introduction of many titles of how various people knew Grandma, all of these titles have one of two things in common that share how Grandma lived her life and why we gather here this afternoon.

The first is that Grandma Guarnier was a role model for all of us through her love for her family. The love for her family of 4 daughters, one son, eight grandchildren, and seven great grandchildren let us all know who we are, and they are her gift and your legacy.

And lastly, today as we celebrate Grandma Guarnier's life, please remember our Grandma not just for the times that you spent together with her. Remember her for the type of person she was. How she influenced your life through her devotion, dedication, love, and respect for her family, and most importantly through the second way of how Grandma lived her life.

As you all know Grandma was a very devout Catholic woman. She lived her faith through her love and dedication to the church, and also through her faith and devotion to God and the Blessed Mother Mary. She tried her best to attend church weekly, she prayed the Rosary at least once a day, and I can't think of a better way to honor my grandmother's life than by all of us remembering her through our own individual love and dedication to the church and God, and by praying the Rosary daily. Through these actions "you'll never forget, and you'll always know, that you honor her everyday in how you live and who you are", and together, as a family, as a community of the church, and as friends we will all remember "In Loving Memory of Margaret Peters Guarnier".

END NOTES

1. <u>Catechism of The Catholic Church</u>. New York: Doubleday, 1994.

2. Lacey, Charles. <u>Rosary Novenas To Our Lady</u>. Woodland Hills: Benziger Brothers, 1926.

3. Johnson, Kevin Orlin. <u>Why Do Catholics Do That?: A Guide to the Teachings and Practices of the Catholic Church</u>. New York: Ballantine Books, 1994.

4. Sly, Randy. "Nine Days of Focused Prayer: What is a Novena?" *www.catholic.org* 14 May 2010

5. <u>The New American Bible</u>. Canada: World Catholic Press, 1987.

6. Holdren, Alan. "After vision of Christ, Nigerian bishop says rosary will bring down Boko Harem." *www.ewtnnews.com* 21 April 2015

7. Saint Louis De Monfort. <u>The Secret of The Rosary</u>. Charlotte: TAN, 1993.

8. "Eucharistic Adoration Quotes Blessed Mother Theresa of Calcutta" stfrancisadoration.org   30 May 2016.

Made in the USA
Middletown, DE
19 October 2021